WHY THE ECONOMISTS GOT IT WRONG

The Crisis and Its Cultural Roots

ALESSANDRO RONCAGLIA

ANTHEM PRESS

LONDON · NEW YORK · DELHI

Anthem Press
An imprint of Wimbledon Publishing Company
www.anthempress.com

This edition first published in UK and USA 2010
by ANTHEM PRESS
75-76 Blackfriars Road, London SE1 8HA, UK
or PO Box 9779, London SW19 7ZG, UK
and
244 Madison Ave. #116, New York, NY 10016, USA

Part of The Anthem Other Canon Series

British Library Cataloguing in Publication Data
A catalogue record for this book is available from the British Library.

Library of Congress Cataloging in Publication Data
A catalog record for this book has been requested.

ISBN-13: 978 0 85728 962 9 (Pbk)
ISBN-10: 0 85728 962 4 (Pbk)

ISBN-13: 978 0 85728 991 9 (eBook)
ISBN-10: 0 85728 991 8 (eBook)

WHY THE ECONOMISTS
GOT IT WRONG

Contents

1

Introduction

Simplistic reconstructions of the history of thought often point to two contrasting views on the relations between economy and culture. The first, attributed to Karl Marx, has it that the economic structure (or in other words, more or less, power relations in the economic field) determines the cultural superstructure, while the second, attributed to Max Weber, holds on the contrary that it is culture, inclusive of religious opinions and doctrines, which determines the economic and social set-up. As a matter of fact, neither of these two great thinkers ever dreamt of establishing univocal causal relations between economic and cultural variables; economy and culture are also to be seen as two vast and internally differentiated categories. Marx and Weber set out rather to establish the relative importance of one or the other causal relation, and did so in strong terms since each was arguing against widespread opinion to the contrary.

The complex relationship between cultural and economic elements is also to be seen at work in the development of the crisis which hit the world economy. In some instances, strong economic interests favoured one view or the other on how the economy works, as a whole or in some particular aspects. In other instances, mistaken theoretical views favoured adoption of economic policies (including a policy of non-intervention in the spontaneous evolution of the markets) which turned out to be far indeed from optimal.

In the following pages, after briefly illustrating the initial stages of the crisis (Chapters 2–4), its immediate causes and its effects, we shall consider the economic culture underlying the choices which favoured the development of conditions of financial and economic fragility (Chapters 5–9). We shall see in Chapter 5 that, despite frequent assertions to the contrary, a number of economists had foreseen the crisis in that they had drawn attention to factors of financial fragility and systemic instability. After all, this is substantially what is meant when we say that seismologists foresee earthquakes: certainly not by indicating the day and hour in which the earthquake will take place or its magnitude, but rather by indicating the areas of greatest risk, so that the authorities can set strict antiseismic building rules for them. We are thus led to look into the specific characteristics of the theoretical views underlying such analyses. In this respect, Chapter 6 will focus on the notions of risk and uncertainty; in Chapter 7, more generally, we shall compare and contrast the two main approaches to economic analysis: the neoclassical or mainstream one which dominated economic culture in the past decades, and the Keynesian (or, possibly better, classical-Keynesian) one. Subsequently, in Chapter 8 we shall briefly consider some issues in economic policy, mainly relating to the institutional set-up of the international monetary and financial system, from a classical-Keynesian viewpoint. Finally, Chapter 9 is devoted to a few remarks on the theme of the relationship between market and state, all too often conceived, especially in the United States, as an all-out opposition between a communist centralised economy and a *laissez-faire* rule of the market.

In depth and duration the current crisis is closer to the Great Crisis of 1929 than to the repeated, and significant, crises of the past sixty years. Even then the economic crisis developed gradually, reaching its culmination some years after the financial crisis broke out.

Opinions differ on the development of the present crisis. Some commentators display optimism talking of a V-shaped crisis – a sharp fall followed by a quick recovery – with a turning point announced for months as imminent, and now seen as passed over. However other, more pessimistic commentators depict an L-shaped crisis, with the fall followed by a rather long period of stagnation (and with a relatively modest short-run recovery attributed to a strong fiscal stimulus which cannot last long). Still other commentators warily stress the marked variability of financial and economic indicators and the differences between countries and economic areas, thus pointing to the great uncertainty in time and manner of recovery. Finally, a number of economists suggest the possibility of a W-shaped evolution, with short-run recoveries followed by new speculative bubbles and risks of public debt crises (since huge amounts of what was private debt had been transformed into public debt), in the context of a stagnating real economy and renewed perilous plunges in the financial arena. Just as in the case of interpretations of the origins of the crisis and the ensuing debate on policy choices, so these forecasts too are associated with the contending views in the economics debate.

Obviously, many things have changed since the period of the Great Crisis. In particular, experience has taught us something about which policies should be avoided and which adopted. Current accounts in the banks (except very large ones) are in no danger, and queues of clients wanting to withdraw their money have been avoided. Unemployment is growing, but it should be possible to keep it within socially acceptable limits (what a horrible expression!), though social tensions are likely to grow. On the other hand, the changes in the distribution of world economic power are remarkable and international political relations need to adjust to them.

Introduction

Policy choices will largely determine how long the crisis will last. The monetary, financial and real policies adopted so far are of proportions never before seen in peacetime. Notwithstanding, the year 2009 closed with a negative growth record in all the developed countries, and with a sharp decline in employment. Moreover, the expansionary policies adopted with remarkable success to prevent catastrophic development of the crisis – the same policies which had frequently been criticized before the crisis as happily forgotten recipes stemming from erroneous economic theories – entail a marked increase in public debt and thus significant risks for monetary and financial stability. It is therefore hard to believe that such policies can be pursued at the present extraordinary levels for more than a couple of years. What will happen when they are abandoned?

The answer we may give largely depends on our understanding of the basic factors leading to the present crisis. According to the optimistic analysts, the crisis may be attributed to certain market excesses and policy errors, but growth may start again almost automatically with no need for big changes in the institutions or the rules of the market economy. It is our contention, however, that the fundamentalist free market attitude, by favouring the tumultuous growth of the financial sector of the economy, has a large share of responsibility in establishing conditions that were conducive to the development of the crisis. Thus, a thorough overhauling of rules and institutions will be necessary if the crisis is not to be followed by a long phase of stagnation, or recovery interrupted by new crises.

The main thesis of the present book is precisely that errors in the dominant economic culture – the so-called Washington consensus – led economic policy to dance blindly on the brink of crisis, and then plunge into it. The myth of an all-powerful invisible hand of the market, the blind faith in automatic equilibrating mechanisms, the hostility to setting rules of the game binding for all participants, the systematic under-evaluation of uncertainty are all, as we shall see, serious mistakes, favoured by their consonance with major economic and financial interests. Such mistakes had already been pointed out through heterodox theoretical approaches such as the post-Keynesian one. Open discussion of these issues is now imperative to avoid the risk of recurrence of the grim drama – not as farce, but as overwhelming tragedy.

Thanks are due to Michele Alacevich, Hossein Askari, Marcella Corsi, Carlo D'Ippoliti, Roberto Petrini, Roberto Villetti and especially Mario Tonveronachi for comments on initial drafts, and to Alberto Quadrio Curzio and Erik Reinhert for encouraging me to complete it. Thanks are also due to Graham Sells for his efforts at improving my poor English. Finally, I am in debt to Paolo Sylos Labini for the many lessons received over the years.

2

The Sequence of Events[1]

Trying to set a specific date for the beginning of the crisis is a substantially useless exercise – an arbitrary choice: it all depends on what we mean by the beginning of the crisis. We may choose June 2007, when Wall Street underwent the first of a long series of falls; or 7 September 2007, when the crisis was, so to say, officially recognised by the de facto nationalisation of Fannie Mae and Freddie Mac, the two financial giants which guaranteed half of the residential mortgages in the US. Soros (2008a) begins his account with the bankruptcy of the American Home Mortgage on 6 August 2007; Morris (2008) goes back a couple of months further, pointing to the fall of two Bear Stearns' hedge funds. But as early as April 2007, the Bank of England's *Financial Stability Report* raised the issue of the sub-prime mortgage crisis and possible contagion effects outside the United States.

If we want to trace the origins of the financial crisis right back, though, we can go still further, to 12 November 1999, when President Clinton (not Bush, be it noted!) ratified the Gramm-Leach-Bliley Act, which drastically reduced controls and constraints on the US financial sector. These measures accelerated the abnormal and unregulated development of the financial, and in particular derivatives markets that played such a major role in the recent crisis. There was a bipartisan agreement: President Clinton, a Democrat, ratified an Act proposed among others by the Republican Senator Phil Gramm, who was the main economic adviser to the Republican candidate McCain in the 2008 presidential campaign; Gramm was also tipped as Treasury Secretary in the event of a Republican victory.[2] As a matter of fact, the deregulation and

---

1 Many reconstructions have already been made of the events of the last few months. Our purpose is not so much to provide yet another account, as to recall the events in order to evaluate the different theories underlying their interpretation. For greater details on the events, here recalled only in outline, we refer readers to the reports of the major national and supranational economic institutes, such as the Annual Reports of the Bank for International Settlements, available online at www.bis.org

2 Financial companies spent more than 5 billion US dollars over the past ten years in electoral contributions and payments to lobbyists in order to promote financial deregulation (Consumer Federation Foundation 2009).

all-out *laissez-faire* stage began as early as around 1980, with Reagan's presidency in the United States and Prime Minister Thatcher's in Great Britain: then the long wave of the so-called super-bubble (cf. Soros, 2008a, 2008b) of the financial sector set in, the bursting of which was primed by the house mortgage crisis.[3]

It is in any case clearly wrong to begin with the bankruptcy of Lehman Brothers Inc. on 15 September 2008, since this should be seen rather as the moment when the crisis reached its apex. Otherwise we would lose sight of the main cause-and-effect relations underlying the explosion of the crisis.

What matters is the intersection of events. Stock exchanges, both in the US and in Europe, fell, losing more than 50 per cent, between September 2007 and February 2009. The fall was irregular, as it always happens on such occasions, with splashes like Black Monday on 6 October 2008, followed in the same week by a similarly Black Friday. A more gradual decline followed, even with some notable upswings or, more often, periods of timid recovery up to what was taken – with greater optimism in the months of mid-2009 – as signalling a change in the trend. Under the surface, however, the difficulties and risks remained intact; stock exchange recovery was not accompanied by a clear recovery of the real economy, where the fall in employment continued.

The fall in share prices differed from one sector to another and from company to company. This was of some importance not only for stock exchange investors, but also because it determined a drastic redistribution of economic power. For instance, we may compare General Motors with Toyota within the car sector, or companies belonging to different sectors such as the financial and electricity sectors. Some countries experienced greater difficulties than others, with a different mix of financial and real crisis. Even if it is too early to identify clear and established tendencies trends, these are important factors destined to produce wide-reaching changes in the global geo-political set-up. Nevertheless, the fall was general: the overall losses of shareowners reached incredible proportions, while slow-downs in production and growing unemployment and social malaise were experienced everywhere.

---

3 Soros (2008b) recalls that subsequently the financial sector grew in importance, as far as representing 25 per cent of stock exchange capitalization in the United States (and 34 per cent of corporate profits, up from 10 per cent on average in 1950–90) and still higher percentages in other countries. In October 1979, under the influence of Milton Friedman's monetarism, the Federal Reserve abandoned the policy of controlling interest rates, shifting to a policy of stabilisation of the money supply; the consequent greater instability of US interest rates, with its impact on international financial markets and currency markets, increased both economic instability and the demand for derivatives utilized to cover risks but also for speculative purposes.

In the first stages of the crisis, many attempts were made to intervene in support of share prices. To begin with came massive doses of optimism on part of the monetary authorities and political leaders, occasionally so exaggerated as to appear ridiculous and counterproductive. Actual interventions by the monetary and exchange authorities followed. The stock exchange authorities resorted to relatively modest but significant interventions on the rules of the game, such as stopping short sales (occasionally limited to some specific share or group of shares, with scant respect for the traditional declarations on the 'level playing field' principle which is an essential prerequisite for real competition). The monetary authorities, for their part, intervened with massive injections of liquidity into the economy of proportions never experienced before. In the meantime, behind the scenes, they sought to favour solutions within the private sector for the rescue of companies in serious trouble in the financial sector.

However, the interventions had only very short-run effects, or even effects that went contrary to intentions. By October 2008, the financial system was on the verge of collapse. Then, when total collapse of the world financial system seemed just around the corner, the governments and central banks of the major countries decided to intervene with the full weight of the tools at their disposal: insurance on current account deposits, very ample financing facilities for the banking sector, offers to subscribe capital in those banks which appeared to be in otherwise insurmountable trouble, active intervention to cover losses in the most difficult cases and sweeping regulatory changes. The means utilized are potentially comparable in magnitude to those thrown into the field on the occasion of the First World War[4]; if they now appear smaller, this is only due to the fact that they are mostly contingent future expenditure, as is the case when guarantees are provided, which translate into actual outlays only if and when sizeable bankruptcies occur.

The stock exchange crash originated in the widespread opinion that a number of listed companies were in difficulty. Initially this was the case mainly of banks, insurance companies and various financial firms. Often, the difficulties perceived by public opinion were real. Besides, since the financial world feeds on confidence, pessimistic expectations rapidly and automatically became self-fulfilling, independently of

---

4 'If we add state aid to credit institutions and emergency refinancing by the central banks in March 2009, we reach a total of 5500 billion US dollars (not inclusive of public expenditure to stimulate the economy). If we take into account inflation, the weight of bank rescues is seven times the cost of the Vietnam War, 23 times the cost of the Apollo space programme that saw America land on the Moon and 47 times the Marshall plan for the reconstruction of Western Europe after the Second World War.' (Rampini 2009, 7; author's translation).

whether the perceived difficulties were real. The worsening of what is called the 'economic climate' soon led to the involvement of non-financial companies in the crisis as well, giving rise to a generalized fall in the stock exchange.

Thus, what to some overoptimistic commentators appeared a limited problem – the crisis of subprime mortgages, to which we will revert shortly – very quickly spread, first from some individual financial entities to all the financial companies, then to the whole stock exchange, and then from the financial sector to the economy as a whole. The crisis spawned a long list of rescues of large financial companies and bankruptcies of minor and middle-sized ones. Occasionally, especially in the first stage of the crisis, rescue operations were launched by other private sector companies; but in any case they came about under the supervision of, or were actually originated by, the public authorities, and in particular the central banks, which often also provided costly support. However, some sensational bankruptcies were not avoided. Once 'too big to fail' resounded throughout the land, now the byword is 'too big to be rescued'.

Obviously, much depends on the economic strength of the potential rescuers. The United States, thanks to its economic standing and the role of the dollar in the international monetary system, can afford interventions which are beyond the reach of other countries, such as the rescue of Citigroup on 23 November 2008. The contrary case was shown by Iceland: when Iceland's economic policy authorities decided to rescue their main banks, it was the whole country that plunged into crisis; when, on 8 October 2008, Iceland's central bank had to abandon pegging of the krona to the euro, the Icelandic currency fell, losing more than 60 per cent in the brief span of a few hours. In subsequent months, thanks to a well organised set of active policy interventions, the situation has stabilized; however, since Iceland imports most of its consumption goods, even a relatively small devaluation, say 10 per cent, entails a loss of purchasing power for the population approaching 10 per cent.

As mentioned earlier, the crisis originated in the United States. From there the contagion spread very rapidly to the rest of the world, affecting both stock exchanges and small and large financial entities. The crisis hit not only Great Britain, whose financial system is similar to that of the US[5], but also the euro area and the rest of the world. The Russian stock exchange also saw a drastic fall, and for some days market transactions were suspended because of excessive falls in market prices.

---

5 At least in so far as the tendency to favour the development of financial markets and the situation of the major banks is concerned. On the whole, the British financial system appears to be characterized by higher concentration and lesser differentiation than the US one and thus more fragile than the latter.

Other countries were also hit, although at least some of them had been far more cautious in their operating practices than the US. For instance, as far as house mortgages are concerned, the Italian practice is to provide loans amounting to 50 per cent, or a maximum of 70 per cent, of the market value of the property, so that even a sharp fall in housing prices does not wipe out the guarantee on the loan represented by the mortgage.[6] In the United States, thanks to deregulation the loan often reaches 90 or even 100 per cent of the price paid to acquire the property; as a consequence, if house prices fall, in the case of non-repayment of the loan the guarantee represented by the mortgage proves insufficient to cover the loss of the financial entity providing the loan. On the whole, also taking widespread consumption credit into account, US families' debts amount to about 120 per cent of their incomes.

The difficulties were not limited to residential mortgages and the financial institutions providing them. Falling stock exchange prices aggravated conditions for a number of investment banks, which often hold stocks acquired through debt. Thus, further difficulties add to the sub-prime mortgage problems.

Since financial institutions commonly operate with a high leverage (i.e. a high ratio between assets and own capital), a relatively small percentage loss in asset values (for instance, just over 7 per cent, if own capital amounts to 7 per cent of assets) is sufficient to render the financial institution insolvent. With a fall in stock exchange prices by as much as 50 per cent over previous maximum levels, losses on mortgages and losses on derivatives (an issue discussed later), anyone operating in the financial sector and directly experiencing the full impact of the difficulties is led to consider all other agents as potentially bankrupt. As a consequence, interbank loans collapse and in their wake all kinds of other loans come to a halt. In this situation, even companies that are flourishing but have short or very short-run debts may find it difficult to refinance their debts and run into a liquidity crisis. (In theory, the distinction between budgetary and liquidity difficulties is clear-cut; however, in practice the distinction may prove more opaque when the valuation of financial activities depends on pressure to sell them at short notice.) Thus, the central banks had to intervene immensely, flooding the market with liquidity to prevent the total collapse of the financial system.

In March 2008, Bear Stearns was rescued by JP Morgan after negotiations conducted by the Federal Reserve of New York and with an ad hoc intervention of about 30 billion US dollars. Staggering as these sums appear, the rescue of Citigroup, carried out eight months later,

---

6 'The ratio between loan and house value in Italy comes to 65 per cent in 2007, lower than the average value for the euro area (79 per cent).' (Bank of Italy 2009, 174; author's translation).

risks costing ten times as much if not more; the cost of rescuing Fannie Mae and Freddie Mac, recalled earlier, or AIG, discussed later, may turn out to be still higher.

In a situation of widespread crisis, interventions in support of ailing banks followed one upon another. However, it is far from easy to act on such a wide front and find the necessary funds. In the first stages of the crisis, a situation which is still not one of panic, rhetorical reaffirmation of the market economy principles, according to which companies should pay for their mistakes, was not lacking. As an example we may recall the initial position of Mervyn King, governor of the Bank of England.[7] With US presidential elections approaching in November 2008, this market rhetoric proved an obstacle to adoption of an all-out bank rescue policy. As long as the other institutions in the private sector could intervene, even if with public aid (which clearly constitutes a violation of competitive market rules), problems could be handled; however, when the need for direct state intervention arose with the private institutions unwilling to take on direct responsibility in rescue operations, then vacillations made themselves felt.

Thus arose the first case in which the US authorities felt unable to intervene: on 15 September 2008, they allowed Lehman Brothers Inc. to go bankrupt. The repercussions were probably greater than expected due to the massive scale of the bank's activities in the derivatives sector and the large difference between gross and net value of outstanding derivative contracts: when the bank failed, the counterpart in these contracts disappeared. Immediately after, however, confronted with

---

7 We may recall the case of Francesco Giavazzi, a professor of economics and the economic columnist of the leading newspaper *Corriere della Sera*. It is illustrated in an amusing book by Marco Cobianchi (2009, 81;91) with a series of quotations. The day after the bankruptcy of Lehman Brothers Inc., Giavazzi (on the web site LaVoce.info, 16 September 2008; author's translation) hailed the event as 'the victory of the market' emphatically adding 'Yesterday was a good day for capitalism.'. Unfortunately, while he was writing these words, the US authorities rescued AIG. Giavazzi then adapted his position: 'This is bad news since it means that the financial situation is still very serious. But it is also good news since it shows that the world economy is in the hands of responsible people who make their decisions without being driven by ideological considerations [...] but only by good sense' (LaVoce.info, 17 September 2008; author's translation). Coming back to the bankruptcy of Lehman Brothers Inc. in 2009, Alesina and Giavazzi (2009) recognize that '*ex post*, it was probably a mistake' not to rescue it. Among the many passages quoted by Cobianchi (2009), we may recall Alesina's excesses of optimism: 'There will be no 1929 crisis contrarily to what Tremonti [the Italian treasury minister] says: what is taking place is a correction like many others', *La Stampa*, 20 August 2007), and again Giavazzi: 'The crisis of the American mortgage market is serious, but it is unlikely that it will turn into a generalized financial crisis', *Corriere della sera*, 4 August 2007, in Cobianchi 2009, 43; 51).

the shock wave produced by an event which was considered nearly impossible, the US authorities decided to rescue an insurance company, AIG, throwing into the rescue means of proportions (according to the press, more than 150 billion US dollars) probably greater than it would have taken to rescue Lehman Brothers Inc. A few days later, the two surviving large investment banks, Goldman Sachs and Morgan Stanley, were transformed into common bank holding entities. This way, US authorities gave the impression that they were intervening case by case, without a clear strategy and the general state of confidence collapsed.

At this point, Bush's treasury secretary Henry Paulson, who held office up to the end of 2008, proposed an emergency plan. Senate and Congress were put under strong pressure to grant it immediate approval without paying attention to the details. However, the very way the plan was constructed could not be considered an irrelevant detail. Paulson, who had come to politics from the banking world and counted many friends there, as well as some enemies, asked for a free hand in the use of an enormous amount of public resources to buy third rate financial assets, reserving himself the right to choose which titles to acquire from which institutions and in what quantity. This was not 'simply' an intervention by the state to absorb private sector losses without any quid pro quo at all. Debatable a choice as this would have been, it also meant that a cabinet secretary approaching the end of his term was being given the authority to drive a gigantic reorganisation of the private finance sector. Decidedly, this was too much and the Paulson plan was not approved. As a consequence, the stock exchange came in for further falls; a new plan was quickly drawn up containing a wide spectrum of minute measures designed to ensure the support of each and all members of Congress. The new plan was on many accounts also less biased in favour of private bankers and was rapidly approved.

The Paulson plan also brought to light a political counter position. On the one hand, we have the extreme market economy votaries, who fear more than anything else state entry into the share capital of private financial institutions, in what is seen (with exaggeration verging on the ridiculous) as a step towards old Soviet-type central planning, and therefore justify any action aiming at avoiding this outcome – even huge gifts to some of the wealthiest and most powerful citizens. On the other hand, we have the liberals, convinced that it is indecent to rescue the wealthy without the community and hence the state receiving something in exchange: for instance, shares to be sold when the situation improves or the guarantee that the managers responsible for bringing the companies to the brink of bankruptcy to be fired.

Everybody knows that interventions to rescue the financial system are very costly and subtract resources from (or utilize resources which had been denied to) social fields such as assistance for the poor, education or health services or aid to the developing countries.[8] However, awareness of this fact cannot mean declining to perform such interventions since a complete collapse of the financial sector would bring the whole economy down with it, and so the whole of society, beginning with its weakest members. Thus, the issue revolved around how to come to a compromise on the scale and characteristics of the interventions: a difficult compromise, within which great importance would be taken on by what were apparently – but not factually – technical details. Here, great attention was called for since the risk existed that the big economic and financial companies might bend them in their favour with the help of their influence over the media.

The immediate collapse of the financial system as a consequence of a liquidity crisis was averted through, among other things, gigantic flows of new money supply into the economy and drastic cuts in the interest rate (including an unprecedented concerted move by six major central banks on 8 October, 2008). The monetary authorities had then to govern what is called retrenchment, or in other words a shrinking of the financial sector of the economy. Substantially, very costly for the private as well as the public sector, punctuated by bankruptcies of small and middle-sized financial institutions, retrenchment is a rather lengthy procedure which may be considered as completed only when the new rules, now under discussion, are enacted – on surveillance, transparency, conflicts of interest, capital requirements and more generally constraints on the dimension of leverage.

With restructuring of the financial sector under way at the beginning of 2009, the policy authorities were already up against another huge and complex problem: how to reform the international monetary system in the face of very serious risks of a debt crisis which could hit many countries.[9] This aspect, as well as economic crisis in the broader sense of the term – namely the fall in production, income and employment – will be taken up for consideration later on.

---

8 In order to convey an idea of the dimensions of the intervention, we may recall that in the European Union 'support to the banking system may reach a maximum of 3000 billion euros, equal to 24 per cent of the Union GDP, inclusive of 2300 billion euros for guarantees' (Bank of Italy 2009, 202; author's translation). Even if we leave out the guarantees, which at present represent only a potential cost, an actual cost of 700 billion euros remains, representing nearly six per cent of the area's GDP.

9 An institutional source, and as such characterised by prudence, like the Bank of Italy (2009, 202; author's translation) recalls that 'worsening of credit quality may continue with even greater intensity over the next couple of years. Further risks stem from exposure towards some emerging countries, since the major Italian groups hold considerable market shares.'

3

The Causes of the Financial Crisis

The immediate origin of the crisis, as is well known, lay in the US mortgage market.[1] US citizens acquired the habit of buying their houses by contracting loans for nearly the full price of their purchase. Often the loan was stipulated even if the borrower already knew that s/he would be unable to pay the instalments year after year: part of each year's instalments would be paid with the year's savings, the remainder financed with new loans. If the value of the house increased, and at least part of the loan was eventually repaid, in the end everything would be all right: 20, 30 or 50 years later, when death intervenes, the heirs come into a property which was originally bought for 100 but is now worth much more, say 200, while the remaining debt from, say, 90 has dropped to, say, 30, paying the instalments of the loan with no need to pay rent for the house. Even if only the interest was paid year after year, while amortisation was financed with new debt, the heirs got a house worth 200, together with an outstanding debt of 90.[2]

The financial institutions providing mortgages had gone through the same reasoning, concluding that mortgages could also be provided to persons who, it was clear from the beginning, would have to fall back on new loans to cover payment of the instalments. If only house prices had kept on growing briskly enough to outgrow the increasing debt, everybody would have been happy. For instance, if the price of the house grew from 100 to 200, while the debt increased from 100 to 150, the wealth of the borrower net of the debt grew and together with income from interest on the mortgage the financial institutions could record an expanding business on their balance sheets. Thus, mortgage providers were induced to boost their business by offering loans also to risky borrowers, and even to disreputable borrowers (the so-called ninja loans: no income, no job, no assets).

---

1 For more information on the mortgage bubble cf. Shiller 2008.

2 In many instances, the greater value of houses has been utilized as a guarantee to obtain new loans for consumption expenditure, such as a holiday or a new car. The financial institutions were happy to expand their business; however, the financial fragility of the economy also increased so much that many commentators expected (and still fear) a consumption credit crisis.

However, many mortgages had been provided at a variable interest rate. Thus, when towards the end of 2006 and at the beginning of 2007 interest rates grew, the instalments increased and a growing number of borrowers found themselves in troubled waters. As a consequence, the ratio of non-performing loans in the housing mortgage section of the financial market grew, also due to the increased share of ninja loans, while the number of new mortgages decreased. This led to a fall in demand in the building sector at a time when many new houses that had been sprouting up when the market was expanding were being put on the market. Consequently, house prices began to diminish.

When this happens, or when it becomes difficult to find refinancing for the part of the loan instalments that cannot be paid off when due, serious troubles arise. Unfortunately, the two conditions are likely to coincide for when house prices decrease the mortgage providers realize that mortgages no longer represent a sufficient guarantee and restrict their loans to the safer clients. People taking on mortgages beyond their means find themselves in deep trouble. Bankruptcy may appear more convenient than continued repayment of the loan when the value of the guarantee diminishes to less than the value of the still outstanding debt. Thus, many mortgages default; instead of the money, mortgage providers get back the houses which constituted the guarantee on the loans (in many states of the US individuals, too, can go bankrupt, not only companies); when the mortgage providers try to sell these houses, their prices are driven down.[3] And there is still more to it.

With the help of financial market deregulation, credit institutions specialized in mortgages had developed techniques of 'bundling', by which they put together many individual mortgages treating them as a single asset. They then transferred these bundles of mortgages to institutions organized for the purpose (the so-called SIV, namely Special Investment Vehicles) and kept them out of their balance sheets. The SIVs had these bundles of mortgages on the asset side of their balance sheet; while on the debit side they had the value of the bonds they had issued to finance acquisition of the bundles of mortgages from the original mortgage providers as a counterpart. The bonds thus created are called MBSs, Mortgage Backed Securities, or more generally CDOs, Collateralized Debt Obligations. The underwriters of such bonds have a credit towards the SIV, not towards the original mortgage provider, and have as guarantee the mortgages underlying the bond issue. If the

---

3 Along with the difficulties experienced by the credit institutions, we should not forget the difficulties of the families often literally thrown out of their homes. Many credit agencies had consciously targeted poor Afro-American neighbourhoods, with difficult access to credit, for the sale of their mortgages, from which these agencies reaped rich commissions. Now these families are financially ruined.

mortgages become non-performing, the SIVs run into losses, possibly to the point of being unable to repay the bonds they had issued (solvency crisis). A liquidity crisis may also arise since the SIVs often finance themselves through short-run indebtedness and thus need continuous refinancing on the market: when the financial markets enter a negative phase, refinancing becomes difficult and/or much more costly. Whether the crisis is of solvency or liquidity, it is the mother house, i.e. the mortgage originating institution, which must take charge of the problem if bankruptcy of the SIV is to be avoided.

The rating agencies considered the risk involved with such bonds as relatively modest on the assumption that, while the uncertainty is considerable for one single mortgage, the so-called law of large numbers applies to a large bundle of mortgages. Within the bundle, only some mortgages will turn out to be non-performers, and in the light of past experience the share of non-performing mortgages may be taken to be small. Moreover, the bond issue can be subdivided into different tranches, some of them with priority claim for reimbursement and/or interest payments, others with subordinate claim. The best, safest tranches obtained a high evaluation from the rating agencies. These were thus the tranches mainly bought by fund managers looking for higher returns than on public debt, when the fund rules drove them to warier behaviour. The subordinate tranches, riskier but with higher returns, were absorbed by the banks themselves and by the more speculative funds, such as hedge funds. Occasionally the process was repeated by bundling together bond packages, thus creating squared CDOs.

On these foundations developed a complex structure of derivative finance products: insurance covers, contingent liquidity lines and guarantees of repurchase of bonds at their issue price. In particular, insurance contracts on the risk of default on the loans (the so-called CDS, Credit Default Swaps) were considered as derivative contracts and issued by 'monoline' companies, concentrating on this line of business and under no obligation to set aside reserves to cover the contracted risks, as is the case, for instance, with normal life insurances.[4] As soon as the first difficulties arose, many of these companies – often, as a matter of fact, no more than hedge funds of minor or average dimensions – went bankrupt: the insurance cover disappeared just when it was needed.

---

4 Originally, before the derivatives market boomed, monoline companies were mainly active in the sector of loans to municipalities. The credit default swaps were excluded from the computation of reserve obligations common to all insurance contracts following the deregulation of financial markets. As a lexical precaution, the artificers of such derivative contracts accurately avoided the term 'insurance' and thus the denomination of default insurance swaps, which would have been more correct.

In practice, there has been undervaluation of the risks in all the areas, from the originary sale of the mortgage down to the derivative contracts on the CDOs, with total disregard for the possibility of a 'systemic' crisis, such as to affect the whole sector rather than a few individual operators. As a matter of fact, in order to determine the proportions between priority and subordinate tranches in a CDO issue, it was held sufficient to evaluate the percentage of a given bundle of mortgages to be considered at risk. If the experience of previous years indicated that non-performing mortgages constituted a small fraction of the whole, and considering that the guarantee represented by the house allowed for recovery of a large share even of non-performing mortgages, a small share of subordinate bonds could be considered sufficient. This way the remainder of the bundle of mortgages could be attributed to a privileged bond issue, which could be considered as risky as sovereign debt. However, taking the experience of the past into consideration did not go back so far as, for instance, the Great Crash, and included only relatively tranquil years that saw no decrease in house prices. Furthermore, reference to past experience meant that a structural change in the situation such as the expansion of ninja loans was not taken into account, such loans having been hitherto practically unknown. The choice of data to be utilized in evaluating risks is unavoidably at least in part arbitrary; however, with automatic application of sophisticated techniques drawn from statistics and financial mathematics the limits to such evaluation procedures and the caution with which their results should be taken remained sunk in oblivion. The results were therefore endowed with a misleading air of objectiveness. Thus, when the mortgage crisis broke out bonds evaluated as safe turned out to be trash assets.

It was these bonds which acted as a link in the chain of crisis transmission by connecting the mortgage sector to the financial sector as a whole, since many credit institutions, not only Freddie Mac and Fannie Mae, had issued or acquired enormous quantities of them. Such credit institutions found themselves in great difficulty, often aggravated by the very complexity of the bundling techniques which made unbundling practically impossible, although unbundling would have cleared the way to limit the area of the problem to the non-performing mortgages, part of which were included in the CDOs considered safe. Moreover, such bonds are exchanged over the counter: not in a stock exchange type of market, that is, with a large number of buyers and sellers ensuring a continuity of exchanges, but in direct relations between buyer and seller. As a consequence, when crisis arose it became immediately apparent how difficult it was to achieve objective evaluation of the CDOs, and even more so of the CDSs. At the first signs of difficulty the prices of these contracts plunged; practically no one wanted to buy them, with the result that anyone who had them among their assets suddenly found a non-negligible part of their assets to be totally illiquid. Moreover, the largest commercial and investment banks held large shares of the riskiest loans, retained when the privileged CDOs had been issued. Furthermore, in various cases the credit institutions had provided guarantees to CDO purchasers, often in the form of contingent credit lines. Finally, they had a considerable amount of mortgages 'under treatment', i.e. in the process of being bundled and transformed into CDOs. The financial institutions more involved in the mortgage sector thus found themselves confronted not only with severe losses but also with formidable liquidity difficulties.

In the situation thus created, the banks which had experienced the same problems but in a relatively minor way, and which could have provided liquidity to the other institutions in greater trouble, found it difficult if not downright impossible to distinguish between counterparts with only liquidity problems, serious as they might be, and counterparts which had liquidity problems and at the same time budgetary difficulties because of losses on the CDOs or for other reasons. Thus the interbank credit market suddenly came to a halt and the general climate in the financial markets grew yet more ominous. When distrust spread, the crisis hit the whole financial system, bringing it to a near complete halt: it became a systemic crisis.

The problem is that the financial system, in the United States as elsewhere, had grown tumultuously and become fragile.

The beginning of this process of accelerated growth – the 'financialization' of the economy – may be located in the *laissez-faire* turnaround which followed, as from 1981, upon the election of Ronald Reagan to President of the United States. To begin with, there was the boom in Leveraged Buyut (LBO), i.e. acquisition of large companies financed with debt.[5] The process of financialization subsequently continued, notwithstanding the crisis of the loan and saving associations and the stock exchange collapse of 1987.

The subsequent stage of financial expansion was characterized by the boom in hedge funds, mainly focused on the segment of derivative finance, as we shall see in more detail later on. Hedge funds operate with a very high financial leverage (ratio of assets to own capital). Thanks to the high leverage, they can reap enormous earnings. If with my own capital of 100 I can borrow 900 and invest 1000 (with financial leverage amounting to 10), and if my investments have a rate of return even only higher by one per cent than the rate of interest paid on the loans

---

5 With leveraged buyout, an economic agent – a physical person or a company – borrows from one or more banks or other financial institutions the resources with which to buy the shares of the company to be acquired, and gives as guarantee the very shares of the company to be acquired. Such shares, it is maintained, should rise in price thanks to better management of the company once acquired.

received, I can earn ten per cent on my capital. At the same time, though, I can lose enormous amounts if something goes wrong: not only if the rate of return of my investments falls, but also if the cost of borrowing increases. Precisely this was what happened with the most renowned of all hedge funds, the Long-Term Capital Management (LTCM) founded in 1993 by John Meriwether, who had among his partners two Nobel laureates for 1997, Myron Scholes and Robert Merton. When the fund plunged into crisis in 1998, LTCM had open positions for more than 100 billion dollars with own capital of only 1 billion dollars: with a leverage amounting to 100, a modest loss of one per cent was sufficient to lose all the capital and go bankrupt.[6]

Commercial banks and investment banks too imitated the example of the hedge funds and under competitive pressures were induced to increase their financial leverage to the extent that in the hottest moments of the crisis, it was much higher than for hedge funds.

Such developments were possible thanks to the deregulation of financial activities enacted with the Gramm-Leach-Bliley Act of 1999 and supported for many years by the chairman of the Federal Reserve Bank, Alan Greenspan. The result was that by the end of 2005, the theoretical value of credit derivatives came to ten times the world GDP and three times the value of all financial products. We must stress, moreover, that the problems stemmed not only from the tumultuous quantitative growth of the financial sector, of which derivatives are only a part, but also from the uncontrolled expansion of its purely speculative component.

Derivatives are complex financial instruments, based on the use of sophisticated mathematical techniques. We have, for instance, call or put options for many kinds of financial assets, which can then be bundled together in such a way as to construct an extremely wide variety of 'positions', depending on the choices of the 'consumer'.

Let us consider an example: an operation of this kind may include the promise to buy shares of a given company A at a certain date, for instance 10 September 2012, for a total price of 1 million dollars, and at the same time the promise to sell shares of another company B at the same date and for the same amount. In this way, there is no need to advance any money, apart from a minimum margin: I simply undertake

---

6 Hedge fund returns obviously display a very wide variability which should be offset by a higher average level. However, the average returns on hedge funds turn out to be lower than is generally believed, due among other things to the so-called survivorship bias (i.e. to the fact that the computations do not include the hedge funds which have been closed) and to the need to rely on the accounts volontarily made public by the hedge funds themselves (cf. Malkiel and Saha 2005). On the history of LTCM and more generally on the financial crisis cf. Morris 2008.

to close two operations of opposite sign (to buy, with a call option, and to sell, with a put option) when the two contracts reach maturity. What I am doing in this way is to bet on the fact that company A will fare better than company B, relatively to what the market believes, whatever the market as a whole will do: the stock exchange may rise or fall, while my bet only concerns the different performance of the two companies. When the contract reaches maturity, it is not even necessary for me to buy on the market the shares of company B which I have promised to sell, nor actually to receive the shares of company A and then sell them so as to receive the money with which to pay for the shares of company B: conventionally, the contract closes with my counterpart paying my margin of gain, if I have won my bet, or with my payment to the counterpart of my margin of loss, if I have lost my bet.

This kind of contract may also apply to bonds, allowing us to enter into bets on the path of long- and short-term interest rates, regardless of whether the whole spectrum of interest rates displays a rise or a fall; or between financial assets of different countries; or between different kinds of bonds (sovereign debt emissions, bond emissions of primary companies, trash bonds) and so on. We may also have recourse to contracts of this kind in order to secure insurance against the risk of specific events. For instance – and it is a concretely relevant instance, since precisely this is the reason why many municipalities, especially in Italy but also elsewhere, now have to deal with heavy consequences from the financial crisis – I can accept loans with a variable rate of interest, which in general cost less than those with a fixed interest rate, and buy derivative contracts in order to ensure myself, even if at some cost, against the risk of an increase in interest rates.[7]

Derivatives can be very useful, both to speculators who can opportunely specify their bets and to agents looking for cover against specific risks. In particular, derivatives can be utilized in constructing arbitrage operations when some financial variables appear to be 'misaligned'. For instance, let us suppose that the rate of interest is four per cent in Europe and two per cent in the United States, while the futures currency market indicates a euro–dollar exchange rate a year hence equal to the present level. In this case, I can earn from borrowing as much as I can in the USA at an interest of two per cent, immediately change the dollars thus obtained into European one-year bills yielding four per cent, and at the same time buy a corresponding amount of call options on dollars (or put options on euros). Then I only have to wait and after a year (or even earlier if, as is likely, other arbitragists enter the scene closing

---

7 For an analysis of the derivatives operations of the Italian local authorities and the consequent potential losses (mostly stemming from the fact that the crisis has seen a fall in interest rates) cf. Sciandra 2008.

the misalignment) I earn two per cent on whatever sum I have borrowed. If I manage to operate with a financial leverage of 100 (one dollar of capital for 100 dollars invested), I get a yield of 200 per cent on my capital. As we can well imagine, with a high leverage, arbitrage operations get under way as soon as an even minor misalignment arises, be it only a fraction of a percentage point. If we add up speculative, cover and arbitrage operations we can appreciate the truly enormous dimensions that derivative finance reached, amounting to a multiple of the value of goods and services yearly produced worldwide.[8]

Confronted with such a dominant role of finance in the economy, Keynes's comment seems appropriate: 'Speculators may do no harm as bubbles on a steady stream of enterprise. But the position is serious when enterprise becomes the bubble on a whirlpool of speculation. When the capital development of a country becomes a by-product of the activities of a casino, the job is likely to be ill-done.'[9]. Keynes continues by expressing doubts on the utility of stock exchanges in directing savings to the best productive investments; he concludes that this is no wonder since the ablest among the speculators have in fact a different target. The viewpoint of financial operators is indeed a very short period (maximizing the present value of assets), while entrepreneurs have a long period viewpoint, especially with regard to decisions on new plant and new technologies, which is the most important element for the development of the individual firm concerned and of the whole real economy. When these criticisms were taken up in Italy by Federico Caffè (1976), a well-known and far from revolutionary economist, they were passed over in silence, treated as extremist notions.

---

8 Over the last few months of 2009, confronted with an apparently unceasing fall in the dollar and with interest rates substantially similar in the different countries, the so-called carry trade has boomed: dollars are borrowed, converted into other currencies and invested so as to earn a rate of interest more or less analogous to that paid on borrowed funds; then it is only a question of waiting for the maturity date of the contracts to convert the assets denominated in euros or yen into dollars, gaining in proportion to the fall in the dollar. Alternatively, it is possible to 'close' the operation immediately by entering into a forward call dollar contract. This is an arbitrage operation, while in the first case we have a speculative operation since betting is on the fall of the dollar. In the arbitrage scheme, it is the counterpart in the forward contract which enters into a speculative operation by betting that the fall of the dollar will be greater than foreseen in the contract itself. In both cases, a financial bubble is taking shape which risks bursting as soon as the dollar ceases falling (cf. Roubini 2009). In the first few weeks of 2010, the dollar increased in value relative to the euro; however, up to now speculating losses from the carry trade did not show up in financial operators' balance sheets.

9 Keynes 1936, 159.

The deregulation started by Reagan and Thatcher and accelerated with the Gramm-Leach-Bliley Act, generated an abnormal increase of the financial sector. This does not mean that rules are wholly lacking. The real problem is that such existing rules are unbalanced – applying mainly to commercial banks and to a much lesser extent to the other financial institutions – and insufficient to counter the risks of a systemic crisis, affecting the whole financial sector and then going on to affect the real sector of the economy as well.

In order to counter the risk of bankruptcy, banks are under the obligation to hold own capital amounting to a preset percentage of their balance sheet assets; the different riskiness of different kinds of assets is kept in account by adopting a weighting system, with weights as low as zero in the case of absolutely safe assets (such as cash holdings, the asset side in the current account held with the central bank or treasury bills and bonds). The rules were established with an international agreement reached under the auspices of the Bank for International Settlements of Basel (a kind of Central Banks' bank); now in force is the second of such agreements, the so-called Basel II, applied in Europe since the beginning of 2008. In order to reach such agreements a number of demands had to be taken into account: those of overall safety, which implied very strict rules and high capital coefficients; and those of the banks, for which own capital is a source of financing more costly than others, with the added disadvantage of making control of the bank itself more contendible.

The logic underlying this approach is that the risks that each credit institution anticipates when markets operate regularly are covered by setting aside specific funds, while the capital endowment constitutes non-specific cover against risks which cannot be determined a priori even as typology. The need for regulatory intervention such as the Basel rules stems from the fact that banks tend to underestimate unexpected risks; hence the capital needed as cover against unforeseen losses. The Basel rules, however, are declaredly based on a micro-prudential approach, since it is assumed that the unforeseen shocks can only affect the individual institution (in jargon, it is an idiosyncratic risk) and not the banking system as a whole (systemic risk).[10] Thus, systemic risk is

---

10 Alan Greenspan, chairman of the Federal Reserve in the period of financial deregulation, well tipifies this point of view: 'All the sophisticated mathematics and computer wizardry essentially rested on one central premise: that the enlightened self-interest of owners and managers of financial institutions would lead to maintain a sufficient buffer against insolvency by actively monitoring their firms' capital and risk positions'. Greenspan seems however certain of these premises since he adds: 'We need not rush to reform. Private markets are now imposing far greater restraint than would any of the current sets of regulatory proposals.' (Greenspan 2009, online).

conceived as equal to the sum of individual risks, with undervaluation of the need to cover against systemic risks.

Furthermore, the banks – especially the larger ones – found many ways around such rules, already not very restrictive in themselves. We have, for instance, recourse to out of balance sheet operations, which imply potential losses not included in the computation of capital requirements, or insurance agreements to cover risks stemming from specific operations, thus allowing for a reduction in capital requirements. The new rules of the Basel II agreement now include out of balance sheet operations; however, the crisis hit the USA while the Basel I rules still held. As far as insurance agreements against financial risks are concerned, not even the Basel II agreement regulates them: in conformity to its basic approach – to leave a discretionary margin as wide as possible to banks – it allows for reduced capital requirements where there are insurance contracts covering risks.[11] However, if – as generally happens – the insurance contracts against risk have as counterparties other subjects within the financial sector, then there is no protection whatsoever against systemic risks.[12]

Moreover, all the financial institutions other than traditional banks, i.e. the banks that collect most of their funds through current accounts, are free from these constraints.[13] As far as the banks are concerned,

---

11 'In the comparison with Basel I we have [...] a significant shift from rules to principles. Due to conviction or to necessity, Basel II relies on two assumptions: that financial innovation rapidly renders each specific rule obsolete and that large financial groups are so complex that any set of rules turns out to be insufficient. Hence [...] surveillance authorities were attributed ample discretionary powers. It remains to be seen how much such discretionary powers really cut into the freedom of action of banks.' (Montanaro and Tonveronachi 2009a, 76; author's translation; cf. also Montanaro and Tonveronachi 2009b).

12 As Montanaro and Tonveronachi (2009a, 68; author's translation) recall, 'at the aggregate level, there can be no mitigation of risks if these are not expelled from the financial system'. This fact should be obvious, but many (both commentators and policy authorities) seem to have forgotten it, possibly misled by the mainstream theoretical view according to which what happens in the aggregate is but the sum of microeconomic events: an idea which tacitly glosses over the many fallacies of composition pointed out by heterodox economists, starting with Keynes and Sraffa, or the fact that in so many instances the crucial assumption of independence of individual behaviours does not hold.

13 To be precise, in Europe investment banks are regulated in a similar way to commercial banks. In the USA, on the contrary, investment banks were deregulated with the Gramm-Leach-Bliley Act, with the result that today no large investment banks exist any longer in that country. Those which did not go bankrupt chose to turn into commercial banks as soon as the financial crisis hit them, in order to exploit the umbrella of the guarantees with which the latter had been provided after the crash.

regulation has differing impact on the banking book (traditional loans and titles held up to maturity) and trading book (financial assets held for shorter periods and derivatives), with a strong incentive to expand the latter. Thus, under the pressure to maximize earnings, financial institutions – and in the first place the banks – took their leverage up to astronomic heights without the slightest consideration for systemic risk.

As a matter of fact, some authoritative figures had spoken out criticizing the very approach underlying the Basel agreements. A number of economists, even mainstream ones, had stressed the intrinsically pro-cyclical nature of the Basel system: when the economy is flourishing, it is easier for the banks to satisfy the capital requirements established by the Basel agreements and financial exposure may grow faster. On the contrary, when the economic climate turns to the worse (not necessarily with a crisis of dramatic proportions), the capital requirements prove stricter and more difficult and costly to satisfy. Thus, the Basel rules favour an excessive expansion of the credit system in good times and an equally excessive contraction in difficult times. The instability of the whole economy is thereby increased.

Other non-mainstream economists stressed a more structural kind of defect, namely the impossibility of measuring risks with precision, due both to the occurrence of rare events for which no statistical information can be collected (the 'Black Swans' mentioned by Taleb 2007: events such as 9/11, the tsunami, a major earthquake) and to the fact that the very structure of the models utilized to interpret the statistical series undergoes change over time. Thus, for instance, to extrapolate into the future the variance of variables such as share prices, stock exchange indexes or the spread between interest rates on Italian and German treasury bills and bonds is but a bet on the future being structurally equal to the past: an assumption which makes sense in fields such as chemistry or physics, but which is clearly devoid of any scientific content in the field of economics. (We shall come back to this very important point in Chapter 6.). Hence, the greater instability and fragility of the financial system which is something different from the 'normal' cyclicality of the economy and a potential source of more serious risks. Moreover, due to the system of incentives under which the decision makers in financial institutions operate, the greater instability and fragility are generated endogenously and thus tend to grow over time.

With an ever-extending web of financial contracts of different kinds in which at least one of the counterparts is a financial institution, the risk of contagion grows when difficulties arise in a specific area of the financial sector. Credit institutions normally have contracts of different kinds open in which the counterparty is another credit institution. Thus, whenever a large credit institution encounters difficulties, all the other institutions with business relations in place get dangerously involved in the problem. What arises here is the so-called counterparty risk: with my derivative contracts I may have gained a large sum on paper, but if the counterparty which lost the bet is unable to pay me and goes bankrupt, I find myself in a tough predicament since I must in any case fulfil my share of collateral derivatives contracts entered into to guarantee myself against some risks. Thus, the credit market ended up like a house of cards: if one falls, all the others follow. It was precisely to avoid such an outcome that the monetary authorities (and when that proved insufficient, government authorities as in the USA) intervened with decision. They could not do otherwise; but the cost for the public purse will certainly turn out to be very high.

4

The Effects of the Crisis

What are the implications of the financial crisis for the families' budgets?

First of all, it is obvious that anybody who bought shares experienced losses, even truly considerable, as did anybody participating in equity funds. The extent of the losses depends on the composition of the portfolios (some shares fell more than others, and in particular banking shares lost a lot of ground). Anybody investing in bills or bonds, monetary funds or bond funds or other assets of the sort should not in principle have lost. On the contrary, with the decrease of interest rates, determined by the more or less compulsory decision of monetary authorities to flood the market with liquidity, they should have gained. Unfortunately, things are not as simple as that and we need to distinguish various instances.

The earlier observations hold true for anybody investing in treasury bonds. For anybody investing in monetary or bond funds, one could expect things to be more or less the same. This is however not the case. We must take into account the fact that fund managers need to cover their costs and earn something on top of that. This means that, if invested 'normally', monetary and bond funds would yield to their clients, net of costs and managerial incentives, less than 'normal' bonds. But anybody entrusting their savings to such funds does this, because the fund managers maintain that, thanks to their experience and ability, they are able to guarantee the saver higher earnings than those obtainable by directly investing in treasury bills and bonds in the market. Yet, fund managers have no magic gifts. Thus, in order to obtain better results the only thing they could do was to buy bonds offering higher returns than treasury bonds – paper certified safe by the rating agencies (institutions calling for some reflection, more on this later on), but which as a matter of fact turned out to be far more risky. For instance, many funds all over the world bought Lehman Brothers Inc.'s bond issues. Once Lehman Brother Inc. went bankrupt, the paper lost much of its value, although when bought it had had AAA rating (higher than that of the Italian public debt!) and fund managers were able to guarantee their clients that their savings had been invested only in safe assets. Many funds held bonds built by bundling together mortgages, as explained above; in this case, too, the losses were heavy.

Obviously, anybody investing directly in such assets also lost out. Moreover, while the fund managers tended to diversify their investments, individual savers did not diversify in many cases, and their losses were heavier.[1]

An aspect worth noting is the resistance shown by many fund managers towards their clients' inclination to get out of the market over the final months of 2008. The argument with which the clients were substantially deceived – no expert would follow it in managing their own funds – was: it is true that prices are falling, but the trend cannot last for ever, and if you wait long enough, sooner or later you will see them back again on the old level.

Why is this argument wrong? After all, this is characteristic of the behaviour of many 'drawer investors' – savers who buy bond or shares when they have some money to invest, then forget about their holdings until maturity or until they need money, for instance to buy a house. But fund managers forget that when they approach their clients to get them to invest in their funds, they make their point precisely by criticising the 'drawer investor' sort of behaviour and offering what they call 'active management' of the funds entrusted to them. Active management consists in selling when a price fall is foreseen and buying back when prices are expected to have reached their minimum.

In the stock exchange, those who earn most are the people able to foresee the turning point for asset prices: an agent with such an ability buys at the precise moment when prices stop falling and are about to increase, and sells at the precise moment when prices stop rising and are about to fall. David Ricardo, the great English economist of the early nineteenth century, was said to have precisely this ability. Obviously, a good speculator is also able to make money by buying when prices have

---

1 The worst fell on those who had retained themselves responsibility for their investments, but followed the (often interested) advice of the bank employees to whom they had to turn in buying and selling paper on the market. In the last few months before the crash, it appears that such advice not infrequently favoured Lehman Brothers Inc. paper in a much higher proportion than would have been justified by the share of such titles in the market. We may be allowed the suspicion that some banks had indicated to, if not ordered, their employees to favour transfer to the bank's clients of those paper assets which were owned by the bank, but that it did not consider safe any longer, as we know was the case before Parmalat's bankruptcy. Without considering this as a scandal, it may be worthwile to verify what happened (which is quite simple for the central banks and/or surveillance authorities by looking at how much Lehman Brothers Inc.'s paper bank held for instance at the beginning of 2006 and how much at the moment of bankruptcy). The regulatory authorities should then consider introducing constraints on such behaviour, going as far as prohibiting bank employees from giving advice to clients who have formally chosen to manage their savings by themselves.

just begun to rise, or just before prices stop falling, and selling when prices have just started to decrease or are about to stop rising. But anyone holding shares when everybody knows that share prices are going to fall is a fool, just like anyone selling shares when everybody knows they are going to rise. With a stock exchange crisis like the one we have seen, any fund manager who kept advising the clients – in September and October 2008 – not to exit from the fund was either not behaving seriously or making a serious error of valuation, attributing the crisis with relatively modest dimensions, much like those of the 'normal' recessions of the past two decades.

Another aspect on which the trumpeters of optimism declaredly relied after the collapse of Lehman Brothers Inc. was the fact that current share prices, considering realized profits, could not but increase since their returns were high. However, as every beginner in stock exchange economics should know, what matters (if any such element matters at all) for the determination of share prices is not realized profits but rather profits expected for the future. In the dramatic situation which the financial crisis was necessarily going to produce for the real economy, it was abundantly clear that the profits of quoted companies were destined to plunge and possibly become losses: the fall of share prices precisely reflects the expectations of falling profits, as is usual in any depression.

Another field in which the crisis has heavy effects on family budgets is that of pension funds. So far most commentators seem to be ignoring the issue, and on many sides we continue to hear advice to remain confident. Such advice comes from the same sources which for years preached the advantageousness of relying on pension funds managed by the private sector, extolling them in comparison to the state pension system. As a matter of fact the pension funds have clearly lost a lot of money: some more, others less, depending on how the fund managers had chosen their investments.[2]

Obviously, in the case of pension funds the results are to be evaluated over a very long time span, so it is correct to say that the negative effects of the recent financial crisis should be balanced with the long and intensive spells of stock exchange growth. However, unless the descent is followed by a very substantial recovery fairly soon, people who had relied on pension funds and will be retiring over the next four or five years will have to make do with much lower pensions than would have

---

2 In some countries like Italy, private pension funds are of relatively minor importance. The problem rather concerns countries where the extreme free trade ideology has greater influence, from the USA to Chile, Hungary, Estonia or Lithuania. In the case of pension funds with investments in company shares, the losses have reached 50 per cent and more, but some funds relying on investments in bills and bonds have also experienced heavy losses (nearly 20 per cent on average in Hungary).

been guaranteed by a public pension system, with returns computed on those of treasury bonds: relatively low perhaps, but also safe.

The issue of pensions is likely to come back under the focus of the economics debate quite soon, when the effects of the crisis become apparent.[3] The arguments that can be put forward in favour of the private or the public pension system are the same that we have heard over the past years. However, perhaps public opinion will now be ready to attribute greater relevance to what to me appears as the main argument in favour of the public system, namely safety against uncertainty. Through investment diversification and the use of insurance contracts, private pension fund managers are certainly able to reduce the uncertainty relating to each specific type of financial investment. Nevertheless, as we have been able to see in this period of crisis, diversification is useless when the whole financial market falls. Undervaluation of uncertainty is, as we shall see, typical of mainstream economic theory. In my opinion, it played an important role in the decision to favour the development of private financial markets, a trend which would be wrong to attribute to the powerful pressure of sectoral interests on the part of financial institutions interested in the enormous mass of funds to be managed, though the existence of such pressure cannot be denied.

The notion that it is necessary to accumulate a fund of savings in order to cover pensions is wrong. In real terms, pensioners' incomes, namely the goods and services they acquire with the money received as pensions, come from current production or more precisely from that part of current production which is not absorbed by the other items of global demand.[4] Therefore, in an equilibrium situation, in which pensioners' consumption demand can be satisfied without engendering inflationary pressures, yearly pension payments must more or less correspond to current pension withdrawals, with the difference, depending on the sign plus or minus, to expand or reduce the public sector deficit. This is what happens with the so-called 'allotment system'. It is precisely this principle which underlies the argument that increases in average life expectancy make it necessary to raise retirement age, too. Analogously, falling birth rates and the consequent population ageing constitute a problem, since the share of old people increases and this engenders a problem of sustainability for the pension system. On the other hand, the

---

3 In the *Final Considerations* of Governor Draghi (Bank of Italy, 29 May 2009) the issue had been recalled, with a declared preference for a mixed system, with a public 'first pillar' and an additional private 'second pillar'. This is a policy view quite different from that of all-out *laissez-faire* theorists, who call for an integral substitution of the public with the private system, leaving to the former only the welfare component.

4 Cf. De Finetti and Emanuelli 1967, 319–20 cit. by Amari 2009, 1114.

so-called 'capitalization system', according to which pensions for each one of us come from pension contributions paid while working, is useful for determining the amount of pension to be paid to each pensioner and as an incentive to payment of pension contributions.[5] Summing up, with a public pension system the computation of what each must receive can follow the principles of capitalization, while macroeconomic equilibrium (namely the equilibrium of the economy as a whole) logically follows the principle of allotment.[6] These considerations are relevant in our context because the development of a private pension system contributed to the expansion of the role of finance within the economy and thus, as we shall try to show, to its instability.

From the financial market the crisis rapidly extended to non-financial companies. It was highly probable that many non-financial companies held 'new finance' assets which would generate losses. Moreover, the collapse of the financial markets led to dramatic liquidity problems which hindered the financing of trade, especially foreign trade, productive activities and investments. This hit firms already under stress in particular, but also those firms which had large-scale investment programmes under way or which for any reason found themselves with considerable financial exposure. Most markedly in the initial stages of the crisis (while subsequently the situation seems to have improved in this respect), the brisk contraction in credit to foreign trade had a strong negative impact on the world economy.

More than these aspects, mainstream theory stresses the so-called 'real wealth effects': since consumption levels depend not only on the flow of current income but also on the stock of wealth, families which suffered losses because of the stock exchange fall are induced to limit their consumption. Keynesian economists, on the other hand, attribute the worsening of the economic climate, and the effect this has on investments, with a major role in transmission of the crisis from the financial to the real side of the economy. This is due to the fact

---

5 In Italy, the problem of fairness in pension contributions – commonly passed over in silence – concerns comparison between the main categories of workers. While dependent workers of the private sector have a strong active balance (given by the difference between contributions paid and pensions paid over the past years) amounting to more than 15 billion euros, other privileged categories have a deficit balance; among these, together with independent farmhands and artisans, we have workers in special categories such as the electricity and telephone sectors and, with a deficit of 3.5 billion euros, company managers. Thus, wage-earning workers contribute to the pensions of the better-off categories.

6 Strictly speaking, this only holds for a closed economy. However, from the point of view of equity the idea that 'young countries' could pay the pensions of 'old countries' is indefensible.

that entrepreneurs invest only if they are convinced that they will be able to sell what they produce. When demand forecasts begin to look unpromising, investment projects are left in the drawer. Investments are the most variable component of national income, or at least they are far more unstable than consumption. A fall has thus multiplication effects: it generates a fall in employment which implies lower incomes for wage and salary earners and as a consequence also lowers consumption.

According to post-Keynesian economists, another element is to be added on top of this: growing income inequality, favoured by the growing role of finance in the economy. It implies a fall (or, if things go well, a slowing down in growth) of consumption demand and this contributes to generating a trend towards stagnation. According to some economists, this element had an important role in the 1929 crisis and – notwithstanding the high propensity to consume in the USA – could have a role in the present situation, too. In any case, the different effects are not mutually exclusive. Economists of different persuasions discuss their relative importance, but they will eventually combine them.

The path which leads from the US financial crisis to the international economic crisis is connected to another problem: an issue long well-known, but one that US policy makers found convenient to ignore. Here, I am referring to the twofold deficit in the balance of payments and in the public sector accounts of the USA, which have cumulated over time bringing internal and external indebtedness to gigantic levels. To this we should add the close to nil saving propensity of US families, with a very large private debt (not only in mortgages, but also in consumption debt, so much so that many feared and still fear a debt card crisis). On the whole, the richest country in the world, the USA, has for years consumed more than it produced.

Considering national accounting identities, the net private sector savings (equal to the difference between savings and investments) always need to be equal to the sum of the public deficit and the current account surplus of the balance of payments. Thus, disequilibrium in one sector finds a necessary counterpart in a parallel disequilibrium in the other sectors. If private sector savings are insufficient to cover investments, given a public sector deficit, we necessarily have a heavy deficit in the current account of the balance of payments. Cumulating over time, each of these disequilibriums engenders a problem which, past a certain limit, proves unsustainable: excessive private debt, excessive public debt and excessive external debt.[7]

---

7 Cf. Godley, Papadimitriou, Hannsgen and Zezza 2007; Godley, Papadimitriou and Zezza 2008. Biasco (1987; 1988) illustrates the real effects of currency cycles, both on the levels of income and employment as a whole and on the internal productive structure of the different countries.

This situation and, in particular, its persistence over time have been rendered possible by the role of the dollar as international reserve currency and the willingness of countries with large commercial surpluses – China, in the first place – to absorb dollars in the form of financial assets (treasury bills and bonds, shares and debt titles of the private sector). Thus, the financial markets increasingly took on the characteristics of international markets, or better supranational markets; the growing role of finance within the economy not only received a powerful boost from it, but also acquired a global nature.

This situation produces another element that is taking on growing importance within the global financial markets, and which negatively influences the possibilities of crisis management: the presence of the so-called sovereign funds. These are state-controlled but privately managed institutions in countries with strong active balance of payment results (from China to the oil-exporting countries). Such institutions are given the task of managing a conspicuous – and gradually growing – share of the currency reserves accruing to these countries.[8] Thus, we have gigantic financial institutions characterised by very low transparency and a mixture of political and economic power that is already giving rise to difficult problems.

Side by side with these effects, the crisis also has heavy consequences for income and employment.

All countries record a sharp increase in unemployment between 2008 and 2009; the rate of unemployment tends to grow to over ten per cent in the European Union, with top levels of nearly 20 per cent in Spain, where the building sector, more sensitive than other sectors to the cyclical downturn of the economy and particularly hard hit by the present crisis, constitutes a wider share of the economy than elsewhere. The slowing down of employment should also be studied in its negative effects on activity rates, especially those relating to younger age groups and women. In any case, we may expect that even when the decrease in income and employment is reversed, the negative effects of the crisis on employment will be felt for a long time. Among other things, in the stage of productive stagnation a reserve of unexploited productivity gains appears within firms, and in the initial stage of the economic upturn such a reserve will engender delays and slackness in the recovery of employment.

The lack of growth in investments, income and employment also implies future losses due to the influence that these variables exert on the productivity path, through the various phenomena of embodied technical progress and learning by doing. In turn, slower productivity

---

8 Cf. Quadrio Curzio and Miceli 2009.

growth implies slower growth in per capita income and so in the citizens' well-being.

Thus, we cannot say that the crisis is devoid of effects on our lives: more immediate and heavy for some, particularly for those who lose their jobs or a significant part of their savings, but also non-negligible and long-lasting for all of us.

5

The Economists who
Foresaw the Crisis

Our account shows the crisis following a logical path, certainly not totally deterministic, but anyhow based on precise sequences of causal links. How is it then that – as so many have pointed out – the economists had not foreseen it?

As a matter of fact, various economists had foreseen the crisis, or had at least pointed out the risks intrinsic to the situation; some had also pointed to the possibility of a major crisis. It was the mainstream economists who failed to foresee it, the supporters of the so-called Washington consensus.[1] They (see for example the book by Rajan and Zingales, 2003) saw great progress in the deregulation of the financial markets and the explosive growth of the financial sector, supported in this by vigorous lobbying organized by the centres of financial and economic power and especially, as we shall see later, by the arrogant dominance – the more arrogant the more distant it was from the canons of scientific rigour – of the various streams of the prevalent neoclassical tradition, based on the idea of the 'invisible hand of the market', namely the ability of markets to find optimal equilibriums by themselves in the long run, if not in the short. The 'heterodox' economists who had foreseen the crisis, on the other hand, did not find their way into the principal newspapers, which are often controlled by the leading financial groups in Italy and in

---

1 The term 'Washington consensus' – originally coined by John Williamson in 1989 – indicated a package of *laissez-faire* reforms propounded by the World Bank and the International Monetary Fund aiming at fiscal discipline, reduction of public expenditure, diffused and moderate fiscal pressure, positive real interest rates determined in the financial markets, exchange rates determined in the currency markets, liberalization of imports, openness to direct foreign investments, privatizations, deregulation and defence of property rights (Williamson 1990; for discussion of such reforms cf. for instance Kuczynski and Williamson 2003). The term, subsequently, took on a broader meaning, indicating the supporters of the dominant extreme *laissez-faire* attitude both in economic theory and policy and is thus analogous to that of 'mainstream economists'; in this sense it includes, as an important though not the only component, those whom Soros (2008a, 74, 91) calls 'market fundamentalists'.

many other countries, or into the main academic journals, controlled in a closed circle of reciprocal valorization by exponents of the mainstream.[2]

Let us briefly recall some instances of economists who had foreseen the crisis.

The clearest case is possibly that of Nouriel Roubini, as much cited today as isolated yesterday within the US academic establishment. Roubini particularly insisted on the risk of the mortgage bubble bursting. But Roubini was not alone, and various danger signals had been also been given some years before, in rigorously constructed analyses – in Italy more often than in other countries, thanks to the incomplete penetration of the Washington consensus here.

In an article published in the *Banca Nazionale del Lavoro Quarterly Review* in September 2003, entitled 'Prospects for the world economy', Paolo Sylos Labini (2003, 179) expressed 'serious worries about the American economy, which strongly conditions the economies of the other countries, particularly in Europe'. Such worries were justified by 'certain similarities between the situation that arose in America in the 1920s – a period that ended up in the most serious depression in the history of capitalism – and the situation that has emerged today'. Sylos Labini (2003, 181) points to 'two speculative bubbles', 'one in the stock exchange, the other in the real estate market', but his diagnosis is also based on the increased inequality in income distribution and the growth of debt, both public and private.

In the December issue of *Moneta e Credito*, in a substantial article entitled 'Crisi Economiche e Mercati Finanziari' (Economic Crises and Financial Markets), Mario Sarcinelli argued his marked scepticism towards the measures adopted or proposed by the economists of the Washington consensus: 'This does not seem the way to reduce the frequency of international financial crises…'.

Six months later, in June 2004, it was the turn of Wynne Godley and Alex Izurieta who expressed serious doubts about the sustainability of US economic growth in an article entitled 'The US Economy: Weaknesses of the "Strong" Recovery', on the basis of analysis of the national accounting balances. A number of papers proposing similar arguments were published by the economists of the Levy Economics Institute, particularly by Godley and Jan Kregel.[3]

---

2 An interesting exercise I might suggest is to evaluate the indicators suggested by so many mainstream economists for evaluating academic research (number of articles and quotations in a set of preselected journals) by comparing the articles in which the possibility of a crisis was indicated with those in which the magnificent and progressive prospects of financial deregulation were extolled.

3 These writings are freely available on the web site of the Levy Economics Institute: http://www.levy.org. See in particular Godley et al. 2007; 2008 and Kregel 2007; 2008; 2009a.

Ex post, many economists have maintained that macroeconomic disequilibriums, in particular the enormous dimensions and the persistent growth of US private and external debt, played an important role in the crisis. As a matter of fact, both favoured the growing role of finance within the US and the global economy, while the big private debt increased internal financial fragility. However, I am convinced that so far the impact of these elements has been indirect rather than direct, which means that the economy still presents enormous potential risks and that it will be difficult to sterilize them. Indeed, the internal private debt could, for instance, lead to the outbreak of a credit card crisis, the external debt to a crisis of the dollar.

Taking an intermediate position between stressing the financial elements and the macroeconomic elements in the crisis, before Godley and the other economists mentioned above, a famous economic historian also known for his studies on the history of the crisis, Charles Kindleberger[4] (1910–2003), had pointed to the dangers of asset inflation (the increase in share prices and real estate prices), maintaining that monetary policy should try to keep under control this kind of inflation alongside – and possibly even prior to – the inflation in the area of goods and services currently produced, precisely because of the risks of crisis which the inevitable bursting of the speculative bubbles implies.

Many of these authors have an intellectual debt towards another great economist, convinced Keynesian and analyst of financial issues, namely Hyman Minsky (1920–1996), considered one of the leaders (together with John Kenneth Galbraith, Sidney Weintraub, Paul Davidson and Jan Kregel) of the American Keynesians.

Apart from the specific characteristics of the financial crisis we are now going through, the mechanisms in action recall the general theory of financial crises proposed by Hyman Minsky in his writings, among which we may single out the 1982 volume, collecting several of his essays, *Can It Happen Again?* (obviously referring to the Great Crash). Kindleberger (1978) utilized Minsky's theory as his own interpretative key for his well-known history of the crises: *Manias, Panics and Crashes.*[5] Minsky's

---

4 Cf. Kindleberger 1995; 2002.

5 This book, as well as the one specifically devoted to the Great Crash, Kindleberger (1973), may be usefully recommended to those extremist supporters of *laissez-faire* who believe that they can attribute the length of the Great Crisis to 'Franklin D. Roosevelt's New Deal which spread doubts on the market economy and suffocated private investments' (Giavazzi 2009, 38; author's translation). Alesina and Giavazzi (2008, 12, author's translation), attribute 'statalistic rhetoric' to President Herbert Hoover, predecessor of Roosevelt, as a premise for attributing responsibility for the present crisis to 'mistaken regulations which excessively favoured real estate mortgages' (Alesina and Giavazzi 2008, 13, author's translation). On the same

theory thus proved useful in interpreting past realities; nowadays it is frequently cited, even by neophytes who do not fully understand its nature and its implications.

It is far from easy to summarize Minsky's theory. Let us, however, try to outline its main features: a theory of financial fragility, a theory of the crises and a theory of the evolution of capitalism.

The theory of financial fragility relies on the distinction between two different kinds of budgetary positions. At one extreme we have the case of the 'covered' position, in which the agent runs into debt in order to acquire an asset, be it real or financial, but his expected income flow is higher, period after period, than the instalments of debt amortization, and the difference between the two flows (expected income and instalments year by year) constitute a sufficient safety margin in the face of possible changes in the situation (fall in income, increase in interest rates in the case of a variable rate debt).

If safety margins are very small, or if it is foreseen from the outset that before the end of the stream of payments and receipts stemming from the investment project the need will arise to re-finance the initial debt, then we have the case of a speculative operation. In this case, even if for a certain interval of time the flow of income turns out to be insufficient to pay the instalments for interest costs and debt amortization, the value of the assets acquired thanks to the original loan (which may be plants and machinery or raw material in the case of manufacturing firms, bonds or shares or other financial assets for financial operators) can anyhow provide the needed guarantee to bridge loans. The speculative nature of this kind of operations lies in a twofold risk: first, when new financing is needed (in the stages, already foreseen originally, in which income flows fall short of current payments) it may turn out to be too costly or too difficult to find (liquidity risk); second, the market value of assets may undergo a negative evolution (market risk).

At the other extreme of the spectrum of financial operations, we have what Minsky calls 'Ponzi finance', eponymous of a famous (or better, infamous) banker at the beginning of the twentieth century. In this case, the asset acquired through debt does not generate an income flow, or does so in a very small measure, insufficient even to cover interest, but it is hoped that the market value of the asset will grow over time at a rate more than sufficient to cover interest payments. Thus the debt has to be continuously (and increasingly since unpaid interest cumulates over time) refinanced. For instance, I get into debt to buy gold, which does not yield

---

lines, Tabellini (2009, 3; author's translation) maintains that 'the crisis has broken out because of some specific technical problems concerning the functioning and regulation of financial markets, and has been aggravated by a series of mistakes committed in managing the crisis'.

any income until I sell it, in the expectation that its price will rise over time at a rate greater than the rate of interest. I run up a debt of 100, and each year I have to add to my initial debt the additional debt needed to pay interest. If gold prices, however, grow at a yearly rate of ten per cent while the interest rate is only six per cent, in the end, when I sell my gold, I can record a gain of four per cent yearly. The total amount of such a gain is proportional to the initial capital I took on loan, so that the more I get as my initial loan, the more I gain. However, if the price of gold should decrease instead of increase (or if it does not display a sufficient rate of growth), I find myself in great trouble, and my creditors with me.

The state of the financial system as a whole depends on the proportion between the different kinds of operations: it is more solid when covered operations dominate, less solid when speculative operations loom larger and decidedly fragile when it is 'Ponzi' operations that acquire substantial weight.

Minsky's theory of crises begins with this characterization of financial fragility. Onto it Minsky builds the following reasoning. Speculators always exist; they become dangerous when their activity expands beyond measure. Hence, responsibility for the financial fragility of an economic system is to be found elsewhere: it is the financial institutions which decide on the extent to which to provide speculators with the funding they require, and it is the regulation of financial markets which addresses their action and sets limits to it.

In their decisions the financial institutions come under two opposite pressures. On the one hand, the more they lend, the more they earn and if they accept greater risks, the risks can be compensated for by correspondingly higher interest rates. On the other hand, they must avoid excessive risks which could bring them to bankruptcy. Thus, much depends on evaluation of the prospects, which should be grounded on a long period view, looking beyond the individual operation. However, such evaluations commonly depend on the economic climate prevailing at the time they are formulated, often affected by a sort of herd behaviour, reinforced by the very short period view of the media – newspapers, television, web sites.

When things go well, the managers of financial institutions wax increasingly confident and tend to underestimate the risks, overestimating the margins of safety. This also happens when they utilize the celebrated risk evaluation models, for – apart from failing to consider the possibility or rather the likelihood of structural changes in the economy – these models utilize data series of generally limited length, sometimes with decreasing weights when going back in time. Furthermore, the context of the financial operators' motivations – competition from other operators, the structure of incentives commonly utilized for determining manager compensations – induces them to focus on immediate returns, losing sight of 'context' risks such as those concerning liquidity or confidence crises, which affect the system as a whole. Thus, not only are guarantee margins gradually reduced, but more importantly the proportions between the different kinds of financial operations change in the direction of greater system fragility. Therefore, when the economic climate comes to a downturn after a sufficiently long period of good weather, crisis can break out with unexpected violence.

As Kregel (2008) maintained, a series of characteristics differentiate the current crisis from the ideal type of Minsky crisis. In particular, Kregel stresses two elements: the powerful boost which the regulatory choices of US authorities gave to the growth of the derivatives market, and so to the maturing of the state of fragility in which the crisis took place, and the role of the persistent deficit in the US balance of payments and consequent accumulation of tensions at the intersection of the monetary, currency and financial markets. However, as Kregel himself stresses, these can be considered additional elements, which reinforce but do not contradict the basic mechanisms analysed by Minsky. Moreover, two other aspects of Minsky's theory appear relevant here: his thesis on the sequence of crises and evolution of capitalism.

When confronted with a financial crisis, as Minsky recalls, the policy authorities intervene to delimit its effects. This implies, crisis after crisis, rescue of financial institutions on the verge of bankruptcy in order to avoid contagion. Financial institutions incorporate such behaviour in their system of expectations on the part of policy authorities. Thus, crisis after crisis, they accept greater and greater risks, relying on the eventual intervention of the policy authorities. If things go well, the profits go to the financial institutions (and their managers); if things go wrong, one way or another the losses are passed on to the public purse. As a consequence, the risks that financial institutions accept tend to grow and the crises take on ever greater potential dimensions.[6] In this kind of

---

6 To rescue a financial institution does not necessarily imply rescuing its management and shareholder value. On the contrary, the two things should be kept quite separate, as happened on the occasion of the Swedish financial crisis at the beginning of the 1990s, precisely in order to avoid favouring the endogenous tendency to a growing financial fragility. However, when last instance loans are utilized or when interest rates are drastically reduced in order to give breathing room to speculative and 'Ponzi' positions, missed bankruptcies translate into an increased financial fragility, which in turn requires further diminutions of the interest rates up to the point when, sooner or later, the bubble bursts (unless the financial institutions in trouble manage to utilize the time thereby gained to increase their income by wielding their oligopolistic power, thus unloading their troubles onto the other sectors of the economy, as has been happening in these months) (Cf. Montanaro and Tonveronachi 2009c).

context the term 'moral hazard' has been often utilized. Though this is a well-known phenomenon, if important financial institutions get into trouble, it is quite difficult for policy authorities not to intervene. This has become apparent once again in the many rescue operations conducted over the last few months; in the case of the bankruptcy of Lehman Brothers Inc. the exception confirmed the rule since the repercussions of the bankruptcy were disastrous.

Finally, Minsky (cf. for instance Minsky 1993) characterizes the development of capitalism as a sequence of stages with very different characteristics: the original entrepreneurial capitalism, the managerial capitalism based on large corporations and finally, in the most recent stage, the money manager capitalism, as he christened it. In the latter, a very short period point of view dominates, quite different from the point of view of the entrepreneurs or from that of company managers, attentive to the long period evolution of markets and techniques. The growing role of finance in the economy is thus seen as a profound change in the nature of capitalism and not as simple development of a specific sector within it.[7] We may add that Minsky saw this evolution not as a progress, but rather (in the wake of Keynes's ideas recalled above) as a factor of decline, to be delimited in its effects through the development of a well-framed system of regulations. We should also note that Anglo-Saxon capitalism went much farther in the direction of the increasing role of financial markets than 'Rhine' or Japanese capitalism since the latter are based on relatively stable financial relations between banks and firms. However, over the past few years, the differences between these kinds of capitalism have been reduced, though not completely annihilated, with a tendency to prevalence of the Anglo-Saxon model.[8]

---

7 In a similar way the French school of regulation locates in finance-driven accumulation a specific 'regime'. Cf. for instance Boyer 2009.

8 On the differences between the different kinds of capitalism there is an ample bibliography. We may recall here Hall and Soskice 2001.

6

Risk and Uncertainty

Minsky's thesis, as we saw, is that financial systems have an intrinsic tendency to instability. In the absence of a strong system of regulation, the growing fragility of financial systems necessarily ends up in crisis, which cannot be interpreted as the simple downswing in a normal economic cycle. This is a Keynesian thesis, in the sense that it stresses both the instability of what Keynes called 'monetary production economy' and that the troubles have to do with the inevitable uncertainty in the evolution of economic and financial variables. In both respects, this thesis is opposed to the one maintained by the followers of the Washington consensus, who see the crisis as having been fuelled by a series of mistaken choices on the part of important economic agents, both private and public, so that recent events do not affect the basically positive evaluation of the stability of market economies. In Minsky's Keynesian view, on the other hand, mistakes are sooner or later inevitable. The risk of systemic crises is always present and must be tackled by setting institutional constraints on the continuous growth of financial fragility and forging intervention tools of adequate strength. From this viewpoint, Minsky's theory and even before that the Keynesian view that Minsky looks back to, imply a marked scepticism towards mathematical techniques of quantitative risk evaluation, which on the contrary supporters of financial deregulation consider an adequate tool against the possibility that the normal downswings in the economic cycle develop into catastrophic crises.

Let us look a little closer into the theoretical problem underlying these different opinions. The distinction between risk and uncertainty has a long history behind it. According to the classical view of probability, from Bernoulli (1713) on, the notion of risk can be applied to those situations in which we have certain knowledge of the possible outcomes and their probabilities. Analysis of risk can then be made applying the mathematical theory of probability, which derives the probability of complex events from the probability of simple events (for instance, what is the probability of obtaining seven as the sum on casting two dice), and concerns phenomena such as a perfectly balanced roulette, a game of cards with a regular pack of cards or a lottery.

According to the so-called frequentist view, the probability distribution can be deduced from past history instead, as we do for instance in the case of life insurance, by looking at mortality tables. This view was reinforced with the use of the Gaussian or normal curve (originally studied by Carl Friedrick Gauss [1777–1855] to represent the frequency distribution of errors of measurement in physical sciences) in the representation of some regularities in the field of social sciences, such as the stature of soldiers. In the economic field, these developments favoured substitution of the term 'normal', utilized by the classical economists, with the term 'natural' in designing the theoretical values of variables such as prices, interest rates and wage rates. It was as if the same 'law of errors' deduced from the measurement of physical phenomena could also be applied to the deviations of the current values of these variables from their theoretical values, with the additional view that the stabilizing power of the market (the 'invisible hand of the market') drives economic variables to their average values.

Finally, according to the subjective view, developed since the 1930s in the writings of Bruno De Finetti (1930, 1931) and Frank Ramsey (1931), the coefficients of probability constitute subjective estimations. Each agent forms a personal set of probability estimates for the different possible events, then the probability theory is applied to establish their internal consistency.

According to the classical and frequentist views, uncertainty is something substantially different from probabilistic risk, even if it is difficult to give a clear-cut definition of it: it includes all the cases in which we have no sure criterion to determine the probability of an event and thus covers a wide range of situations. In any case, both the classical and the frequentist theories of probability exclude uncertainty from their field of analysis. In the case of the subjective approach, on the other hand, we can form estimates of probability for any event whatsoever by assuming that the agent is willing to bet in favour or against the event, thus revealing his/her personal evaluation. A market for bets can then generate for each event an average value for the probability coefficient. In this way, the kind of uncertainty which cannot be reduced to probabilistic risk – a kind of uncertainty which is a basic component of the world we live in – can also be reabsorbed into the field of probability theory, at least in principle.

Thus, uncertainty has been relegated at the margins of economic theory, as a complication which we can in any case take into account. Among those who considered it explicitly, within the marginalist approach, we may recall Frank Knight, one of the major US economists of the first half of the twentieth century, commonly considered one of the founders of the Chicago School. According to Knight (1921), writing before the birth of the subjective approach to probability, the distinction between the two notions, risk and uncertainty, is given by the fact that risk can be assimilated to a specific kind of cost, namely the payment needed to insure against it; while uncertainty is the domain of the estimates and intuitions of the expert. As a result, Knight was able to put forward an interpretation of/justification for the existence of profits: defined as residual income once the payments for the factors of production have been deducted (including the interest on capital advanced), profits are considered remuneration for entrepreneurs' ability to take the right decisions under conditions of uncertainty. Thus, an entrepreneur earns profits if s/he is better than the average economic agent at managing things in a complex world, while facing losses if below average. Theoretical study of the normal conditions in the functioning of the economy can therefore ignore uncertainty (*ex-ante*) and profits (*ex-post*), taking only risk into consideration.[1]

Later on, in the decades following the Second World War, first in the United States and then in the rest of the world, the subjective theory of probability came to dominate in the economic field, too, thanks to the writings by Savage (1954) in the area of statistics and by von Neumann and Morgenstern (1944) in that of economics. The latter approach has been taken up in the pure theory of general economic equilibrium, with the expected utility theory, as it is known, in which each agent, together with a specific set of preferences, also has specific expectations of the future, organized in a coherent scheme.

According to the subjective approach, probability evaluation is effected by the agent and is revealed through his/her choices. Probability theory assumes as given the subjective distributions of probability manifested by each subject through their own actions and keeps for itself the task of analysing the implications of such distributions, on the basis of the assumption of internal consistency of the choices of each individual. In this way, algebraic manipulations of subjective probability distributions can follow the same routes as classical probability calculus.

Keynes's approach is different.[2] Just how radically it differs from the subjective approach is still a debated issue. Keynes himself entered into controversy here with Frank Ramsey, a student of his and one of the founders of the subjective school; but when Ramsey died (aged 30), Keynes (1931) expressed a conciliatory view in his obituary. As we have seen, Keynes had set out his theory in a book published in 1921 to which he had devoted much time. An early draft is dated 1908, as a dissertation submitted for a Cambridge King's College fellowship. The dissertation was then revised in the following year and subsequently developed in book form.

---

1 Knight's theory has often been misinterpreted and referred to inappropriately. Cf. for instance Cooper 2008, 145–6.
2 For more on Keynes's probability theory, cf. Roncaglia 2009b.

Keynes developed a theory of probability intermediate between the subjective and objective approaches. In his opinion, it is true that agents have a central role in estimating the probabilities of real events, but we should also recognize that such estimates largely depend on reality itself. In relating themselves to reality, agents can distinguish three kinds of situations: those in which the evaluation is certain, even when it ends not with definite events but with probability distributions, those in which it is possible to provide quantitative estimates of probability and those in which no definite evaluation can be expressed. The first kind of situations includes sure events (there is at least one railway station in Rome and at least one in London) or for which there is a sure probability distribution (lotteries, which we assume not to be rigged). The second group of events covers phenomena for which reasonable evaluations of probability can be formulated; for example, only 20 per cent of trains from Rome to Milan in the past year showed a delay over ten minutes. Thus, if I travel on one of these trains, I have a four out of five probability of arriving more or less on time. The third group of events is wholly impermeable to evaluations: how could I evaluate the probability that whoever the president of the United States will be in 2130, he/she will be between 30 and 40 years of age? As a matter of fact, I do not even know whether the United States or its institution of presidency will still exist. Obviously there are many intermediate possibilities; the three cases illustrated above merely constitute a typology for our analysis. In this respect, Keynes suggested a notion, 'confidence in the estimate of probability', to flank the notion of probability. Confidence simply indicates how much I think I can rely on my estimate. When the state of my knowledge changes, I can revise both my evaluation of the probability of a given event and the confidence I have in my estimate: after reading a promising weather forecast, I can revise my estimate of the probability that the Rome-Milan train will be more or less on time from 80 to 85 per cent and at the same time have more confidence in my evaluation since I have been able to take into account an additional element, and am therefore convinced that there is no chance of bad weather delaying my train.

Let us stress some aspects of this approach. It is clear that Keynes not only substitutes Knight's dichotomy between risk and uncertainty with a more complex position in which probabilistic risk and absolute uncertainty (or complete ignorance, as Keynes prefers to say) constitute the two extreme cases, while 'partial' uncertainty corresponds to the by far greater majority of real-world situations. In contrast with the subjective approach, Keynes stresses that probability estimates cannot simply be assumed as given: the social scientist must work on them. Moreover, and especially, it is not possible to have a complete distribution of probability over the whole 'space of events', i.e. the set of possible events. As a matter of fact, it is the very notion of space of events which must come in for critical consideration when I have to do with real-world events and not abstract models. If I am speaking of casting a real die, I cannot stop at the six theoretical events consisting in having as outcome one of the six faces; the die may happen to be disintegrated by a laser ray in mid-air, disappear in a manhole or a thousand similar possibilities. While events of this kind are sufficiently unlikely in the case of a die for us to discard this possibility, in the case of the normal events of life it is always possible for something unexpected to happen. Moreover, in real life, something wholly unexpected always happens sooner or later.

What is the point in discussing an issue like this at some length? The point is that the theory of probability utilized in developing and pricing the new financial derivatives relies on an approach which is half-way between the classical-frequentist view and the subjective view, and is very far from the Keynesian perspective. On the one hand, consistently with the subjective approach, the values expressed by the market for the main financial variables like stock exchange prices or the maturity structure of interest rates are considered as the average expression of financial agents' expectations. Arbitrage operations, which take up a large share of current activity in the derivatives sector, are based on the assumption that the systems of expectations of financial agents are internally consistent, thus allowing for the utilization of the mathematical theory of probability. On the other hand, the estimate of risk intrinsic to different operations and hence the price to be attributed to different options (call, put or complex combinations of these two basic categories in relation to different maturity spans and different assets) is made with recourse to the frequentist approach, by considering the variability (the variance, in statistical terms) shown in the past by financial variables (interest rates, stock exchange prices and so on).[3]

In this way, recourse to the traditional approaches to probability allowed for the utilization of apparently rigorous techniques, which should have prevented not so much isolated cases of losses and bankruptcies, intrinsic to the speculative character of financial markets (leaving aside the ever-present possibility of individual errors in the utilization of so complex tools)[4], but rather cases of general crises. The real issue, however, rests on whether the traditional notions of probability are applicable to the

---

3 The contradiction deriving from the joint utilization of two different approaches to probability is reinforced by the fact that the new finance has the presumption to utilize historical series concerning the past movement of the variables of interest in a context which is continuously modified by the very introduction of the new financial instruments.

4 However, this aspect should not be exaggerated. A good manual of financial mathematics provides all the necessary tools and is no more difficult than a textbook on quantum physics or on Kant's ethics.

case of the financial markets or whether the Keynesian approach to probability should rather be preferred. In this latter case, we should consider what differences this implies for interpretation of the working of financial markets and choice of the appropriate regulation system.

The Keynesian view of uncertainty brings to the fore the difficulty of defining the space of events. The case of a laser ray hitting the die in mid-air is clearly a joke and may be left aside, but history is full of unexpected events, big and small, from the discovery of penicillin to the destruction of the Twin Towers. The future is always full of surprises. Past experience, in particular time series for financial variables, may possibly constitute a reasonable guide when things are going smoothly, but we should know that periods of tranquillity never last for ever.[5] On the contrary, in the economy there are always some endogenous structural change processes at work (for instance the tendency to increase in financial fragility pointed out by Minsky, discussed earlier), so that the assumption of stationarity is most certainly misleading, whatever the aspect of economic life to which it is applied.

In a sense, financial market operators acted as if risks only came from individual cases of deviation from the normal behaviour, as if the different events (bankruptcy of mortgage holders A and B, interruption of electrical services, an accident in a manufacturing plant) were independent of one another, while in many instances this is not the case. Thus, not only the financial operators, but also the policy authorities regulating the working of the financial markets, forgot or at least drastically undervalued the possibility of systemic crises.

In other words, the problem lies in the erroneous sensation of 'certainty' (in the technical sense of the word) granted by recourse to the techniques of stochastic analysis and financial mathematics in building operations in derivatives. When confidence in such techniques translates into a reduction of the guarantee margins (which, as we have seen, constitute a cost for financial operators), negative unexpected events, the possibility of which had not been taken into account, may blow up into gigantic crises.

---

5 The impossibility of defining exhaustively the space of events implies the impossibility of utilizing the theory of general intertemporal economic equilibrium of the Arrow-Debreu kind to maintain that uncertainty could be completely eliminated if only there were a sufficient number of contingent markets (one for each commodity, each interval of time and each 'state of the world'). Unlike so many ex post assertions, the under evaluation of risks to which at least part of the responsibility for the crisis is attributed is not 'a trivial error of evaluation' due to the 'difficulty of correctly evaluating the probability of rare and infrequent events' (cf. Tabellini 2009, online, author's translation), but the unavoidable consequence of out-of-place utilization of a specific theory of probability and the economy.

Arguments of this kind are not new. In his book *The Black Swan* (2008), Taleb – a financial operator with an excellent personal record in the job – illustrates an analogous argument. George Soros, another financier of outstanding success, proposes in various writings (among which we may recall Soros 1999; 2002; 2008a; 2008b) the notion of 'reflexivity': financial markets provide a commonly distorted evaluation of economic reality – in some stages over-optimistic, in others over-pessimistic – and the market prices formed on such a basis in turn influence the 'fundamentals', i.e. the main characteristics determining the evolution of the economy. Thus, we have a bidirectional cause and effect nexus between reality and the financial agents' evaluations – Soros' reflexivity – which in some circumstances may give rise to a cumulative spiral, leading to crisis.[6]

Unfortunately, subservience to mainstream economic culture induced the majority of commentators to consider all arguments of this kind 'external to true science', represented by Nobel prize-winning authors of financial mathematics for derivatives pricing, of publications in the 'more prestigious journals' (i.e. characterised by a high level of mathematical sophistication, though with little if any attention at all to the plausibility of the basic assumptions), of career selections and research financing oriented to the mainstream canon. A good research policy should leave adequate room for non-conformists; in any case, their arguments should be considered on their merits and not rejected apodictically or worse totally ignored, as happened in so many instances in the debates on the deregulation of financial markets.[7] One can only hope that the lessons of the present crisis will be kept in consideration in the future.

Indeed, the assumed objectivity of the techniques of the new derivatives finance is precisely what constitutes their main appeal. For agents working in financial markets, and in particular for managers of other people's wealth, it is much better to be able to operate with complex techniques (which thus justify exceptional earnings) which should make risks measurable and allow for stipulation of insurance

---

6 The critiques illustrated here are different from those which, within the framework of the mainstream approach, concern an error in the evaluation of the probability distributions which could have 'fat tails'. What Taleb (2008, chapter 16) maintains (and, as he himself recalls there, before him also Benoit Mandelbrot, the theoretician of fractals), is that recourse to the assumption of a 'normal' distribution is most often unjustified.

7 For instance, in their long book supporting the most complete deregulation of financial markets, Rajan and Zingales (2003) succeed in never referring to authors such as Minsky, Kindleberger, Galbraith, Kregel, Godley, Sylos Labini and so on (Keynes is named, but without providing any bibliographical reference and ignoring his main theses concerning the argument dealt with).

contracts against the possibility of negative events. In this situation, the income of financial institutions can be interpreted as remuneration for greater technical ability, as well as fruit of arbitrage between clients with different needs and different attitudes towards risk. Ample margins of profit are in fact possible thanks to the undervaluation of all kinds of risk, on the part of both the financial institutions and the rating agencies (which in the wake of gigantic conflicts of interest had gone so far as to certify Lehman Brothers Inc. as being safer than the Italian treasury) and especially thanks to the deregulation of the financial markets – which allows firms working on derivative finance not to bear excessively high costs for the capital reserves – which would have been needed as cover against systemic risks. In this way, as long as things go well, firms operating in these markets can earn incredible sums (even if those erring in construction of the derivatives castles may lose out, but these are considered technical errors, much like the errors of an engineer in computations for the construction of a bridge and not the entrepreneurial risks so often mentioned in the press). If things go wrong, the resulting crisis may turn out to be so big as to require state intervention with the state taking on responsibility for all the costs.

This is what happened in the case of the LTCM crisis in 1998 mentioned earlier, and this is what is happening now (ironically enough, one of the many interventions concerns apparently the activities of the ex-boss of LTCM, Meriwether, back again to operate for incredibly large sums in the very market from which he had to exit in such a shameful way.).

7

The Crisis of Economic Culture: Neoclassical Candides and Keynesian Voltaires

The prevailing opinion among mainstream commentators is that the financial crisis may have negative effects on the real economy (it is hard to deny what is evident!), but relatively limited and soon to be absorbed, with the turn-around commonly foreseen within the following six to12 months (some Nobel laureates were already forecasting this in 2007!), if not already over and done with. Some commentators add that crises provide an important contribution to the proper functioning of the market economy; frequently recalled in this respect is Schumpeter's (1912) thesis of 'creative destruction'. This has to do with the fact that bankruptcies constitute a selection tool by which the market economy eliminates the incapable, leaving room for the more able entrepreneurs.

This is a thesis as much cited as little understood, especially with regard to its analytical prerequisites. Indeed, Schumpeter bases his reasoning (as neoclassical theory, which is at the heart of modern mainstream economic culture, commonly does) on the assumption that the market is capable of ensuring the full employment of resources, workers included – an assumption that, as we shall see in more detail later, is a central result of the neoclassical theory of value and distribution, but that has already come in for destructive criticism on the part of Keynes and Sraffa. When introducing an innovation under conditions of full employment, the entrepreneur needs to subtract resources from their customary use in order to realize it; this is possible thanks to the banks' finance, paying for resources at a higher price but all the same succeeding in earning profits thanks to innovation. Gradually, the technical improvement is imitated and anyone falling behind in the innovative process, hamstrung by tradition, will fail to cope with the increase in costs due to the rising prices of means of production and follow the path to bankruptcy. Thus, firms going bankrupt free resources that can be utilized more efficiently by innovators and imitators. The change characterizing capitalistic development therefore implies a succession of stages of growth and stages of crisis, with a cyclical path in which the negative stages are the unavoidable complement to the positive stages. On the whole, technical progress and the redistribution of resources from less efficient to more efficient firms ensure the growth of production and income in the long run.

This theory includes four characteristic elements: the heroic view of the entrepreneur who introduces innovation by breaking with the past, the central role of the banker in the process of development since it is the banker who selects the innovations to be realized and thus allows and directs the development process through his/her far-sightedness and his/her judgement of persons and situations, the assumption, mentioned earlier, of full utilization of resources and finally innovations seen as a process of rupture of the existing equilibrium. The first and second element had notable influence in favouring the spread of Schumpeter's theory. However, they depend on the third and the fourth which constitute the weak points of this theory.

The approach viewing innovations as a rupture of the pre-existing equilibrium is opposed to the view of the innovative process developed by Adam Smith (1776) and his successors, like Charles Babbage (1832). Smith and Babbage stress the growing division of labour, the introduction of new means of production, learning on the side of workers and rationalization of the productive process. Innovations and technical progress are viewed as a natural activity ever at work within a market economy. In the framework of Nicholas Kaldor's theory (one of the many great economists who did not receive the Nobel prize)[1], investments in fixed capital to replace old machinery regularly embody technical improvements, which are thus at least in part financed by the amortization normally set aside by the firm.[2]

The assumption of full utilization of resources is a traditional feature of neoclassical theories, based on the 'laws' of supply and demand. According to the traditional representation of the market process, whenever supply overtakes demand, the price is driven downwards. This provokes an increase in demand (and, in some instances, a fall in supply); the price decrease only stops when demand and supply are equal. The traditional neoclassical approach also applies this theory to the so-called 'factors of production': land, capital and labour. Whenever there are unemployed workers in a competitive labour market, the wage rate is

---

1 See for instance Kaldor and Mirrlees 1962.
2 Obviously, this does not imply the non-existence of major innovations, such as to involve changes in the 'technological paradigm', like for instance the invention of the steam engine or the development of information technology. Indeed, such innovations have great importance in economic development. However, it would in any case be wrong to study such processes adopting the assumption of full employment of resources.

driven downward. This induces firms to hire more workers. Hence, responsibility for unemployment should be attributed to trade unions and to all the other 'imperfections' which distance the labour market from perfectly competitive conditions.

However, in the wake of criticisms by Keynes, Sraffa and their followers, modern theory had to recognize that the neoclassical theory described before suffers from irreparable defects and is to be abandoned. Keynes pointed out that what unemployment pushes downward is not the real, but the monetary wage rate: if prices fall, then the real wage may remain unchanged. In any case, the fall in wages implies a fall in aggregate demand, and so a worsening of the economic climate, which in turn causes a decrease in investments as well with further increase in unemployment. Moreover, as we shall see in more detail further on, the rate of interest is not determined by supply of and demand for loanable funds (i.e. with some simplification savings and investments) either, and therefore it cannot contribute to bringing the economy towards equilibrium. Sraffa (1960, chapter 12) adds to these critiques a more complex consideration concerning the link between the wage rate and the 'capitalistic intensity' of productive processes, namely capital per worker, showing that a fall in the wage rate does not necessarily lead to utilization of more labour-intensive techniques and thus an increase in the use of labour. The more sophisticated neoclassical theory, that of general economic equilibrium, has recognized the multiplicity and potential instability of equilibriums, which means that the thesis of an automatic tendency among competitive markets towards full utilization of resources is devoid of scientific foundations, even within the marginalist approach itself.[3]

In modern mainstream macroeconomics, these difficulties are solved in the simplest – but also scientifically less serious – way, namely by leaving them aside. It is a now consolidated custom for mainstream theoreticians to focus on the analysis of equilibrium conditions, without taking the trouble to establish whether the economy is attracted to them or, on the contrary, tends to move along other and possibly diverging paths. On the contrary, it is considered bad taste to 'waste time' on such issues, leading to such inconvenient results. Notwithstanding, interpretations of what happens in the real world and economic policy recipes are presented as if based on scientific laws, sure and verified, while the foundations of such laws are a mere quagmire.

By the way, in Schumpeter's theory there is another assumption which fails to find confirmation in current events. Schumpeter's idea is that in

---

3 Here we can only recall in broad outline a wide-ranging and complex debate. These are in any case well-known issues, illustrated in a great many books and articles. Cf. for instance Harcourt 1972; Tonveronachi 1983; Roncaglia 2001; 2009a.

the course of crises the entrepreneur or banker who loses, has to exit the scene. Schumpeter himself experienced such a situation in 1924, when the Biedermann Bank, of which he was chairman, went bankrupt: not only did he lose all his savings, but also, for a number of years, he had to go on paying the debts incurred from his salary as university professor. In the current situation, not only public aid assists entrepreneurs and bankers and the owners of financial firms that have either gone bankrupt or would have, without public support. Moreover, given the short-run view within which the rich bonuses of financial managers are decided upon, the managers responsible for disastrous choices, even when they lose their jobs, find themselves with cumulated earnings far superior to the salaries of a whole working life of qualified workers such as engineers working in firms or researchers in biotech companies. The 'punishments' of the crisis tend to fall mostly on innocent people, including those – like researchers – who may be considered the real artificers of technical change and hence of economic and social progress.[4]

Therefore, crisis is not an essential precondition for technological progress. On the contrary, various elements suggest the opposite relationship. Firstly, in relatively prosperous periods it is easier to finance research, both for the public purse and for the private sector. Secondly, when the economy grows, it is necessary to invest in order to increase productive capacity and production, and to this end commonly new machinery is bought embodying innovations (the so-called embodied technical progress). Thirdly, when the size of the economy grows there are, at least up to a point, savings of many different kinds to be reaped (the so-called economies of scale, even dynamic ones as in the case of learning by doing) which also constitute an important element of technical progress. In periods of crisis, on the other hand, investments stagnate, and the firms in trouble cut all expenses not immediately essential, beginning with research investments; the same practice is followed by governments.

The thesis that necessity stimulates ingenuity is centuries old, proposed by reactionary and conservative intellectuals of all epochs and has been criticised for centuries by progressive intellectuals.[5] Especially in the

---

4 The earnings differential between employees in the banking and financial sector and researchers in the private and public sectors largely depends on the oligopolistic nature of the former: as Sylos Labini (1984, 187) remarks, oligopolistic extra-profits are commonly transformed into extra-income for subordinate workers within the sector, too. This differential constitutes an incentive distorting preferences in the choice of the course of study, the career and life styles which over the long period may have heavy negative effect on scientific and technological progress, economic development and so on.

5 Baron Necker, the last minister of finance of King Louis XVI before the Revolution, supported this kind of idea, opposing progressive economists such as Turgot, Condorcet or Adam Smith (Cf. Rothschild 2001).

more qualified jobs, relative tranquillity is conducive to productive work. Entrepreneurs anxious to keep afloat are primarily concerned with their accounts and finding the liquidity needed to get over the difficult period, and can only postpone any research and development projects.

At least with respect to the present crisis, it is therefore utterly out of place to speak of 'creative destruction': even if normal cyclical oscillations may help the economy to get rid of the less efficient firms, the loss of income and employment brought about by the crisis rather constitutes an obstacle to the progress of scientific knowledge and technology and a source of severe suffering and social tensions.

Another ruse adopted by mainstream theory to sweeten the crisis pill consists in considering it as an exclusively short period phenomenon. We are thus lectured about a long period growth path, around which oscillations take place: downwards in periods of crisis, upwards in boom periods. Upward oscillations compensate, nay more than compensate, for downward oscillations. Growth of the economy in the long period is thus determined by the so-called 'fundamentals': the share of savings over income, which over the long run allow for the financing of a corresponding share of investments, and technological change, which is considered as being external to the field of analysis of the macroeconomists, as if it depended on 'God and the engineers'. Thus, economic growth turns out to be constrained by the availability of resources; as we saw before, the invisible hand of the market should ensure – in the long, if not the short run – the full utilization of available resources, hence growth at the pace made possible by the gradual accumulation of new resources and technological change. In order to ensure the smooth functioning of the invisible hand of the market, 'structural reforms' are supported, ranging from a reduction in the role of the welfare state or the public education system to a reduction of the bargaining power of workers through changes in the industrial relations set-up ('boosting competitiveness in the labour market').

This approach shows two crucial, interconnected weak points in addition to the point about the ability of the market to ensure full resource utilization discussed earlier. The first lies in the assumption of a given quantity of resources, the second in the idea that the real evolution of the economy does not affect its growth potential in the long period. In modern economies, scarce resources do not only include natural resources (which as a matter of fact are never fully utilized: instances in which such a situation is approached, such as fresh water for cooling industrial and electricity plant in England or in Saudi Arabia, are commonly treated as specific issues, different from the common ones of growth). Above all, there are circulating and fixed capital inputs (plant and machinery, raw materials and intermediate products). However, these are goods which can be produced and

53

therefore cannot be considered as absolutely scarce. In fact, they can be considered scarce only when it is impossible to increase their production – when, for example, the plants producing them are 100 per cent utilized, when it is impossible to find new workers for hire, or when no land can be found to install the new plant or machinery. However, this is never exactly the real-world situation. Only in wartime has there been a real scarcity of workers (also due to the fact that migration becomes impossible). There is always some flexibility in plant utilization (for instance with recourse to night or holiday shifts); again, only in wartime has the production of commodities, such as steel, met with real bottlenecks in available productive capacity.[6]

It is the strength of the ideological tradition which emboldens economists to embrace the viewpoint of scarcity. It is common to say that economics studies choice between alternatives when the endowment of resources is scarce. The market is conceived as a point in time and space where demand and supply meet, as in the case of the medieval fair, or of today's stock exchange, although it is paper titles rather than commodities that are exchanged there. This is a view which dates back from classical antiquity and now dominates within mainstream economics. However, it is not the only approach open to us. Between the seventeenth and the nineteenth centuries the 'classical' economists such as William Petty, François Quesnay, Richard Cantillon, Adam Smith, David Ricardo, James and John Stuart Mill and many others indeed followed a different route, taken up recently by Piero Sraffa and some of his followers. This approach analysis of the economy focuses on the division of labour and thereby on the continuous production and reproduction of means of production and consumption which are exchanged between the sectors making up the economy which never works in an optimal way (according to the Enlightenment view of Smith and Kant, society is not a perfect system, nor are human beings perfect, compared to 'coarse clay' or 'crooked sticks').[7] The aim in studying the 'wealth of nations' (which by and large corresponds to per capita income) is to explain why some countries are richer than others. The explanation is found in the

---

6 The idea that the availability of new workers corresponds to the number of the unemployed is misleading since it leads to a drastic underevaluation of the potential of the economy (cf. Roncaglia 2006). In the Italian case, in order to illustrate this point it is sufficient to compare the rates of (male and especially female) employment in the southern and in the central-northern regions: 68 per cent versus 77.9 per cent for males in 2008, and 37.2 per cent versus 59.7 per cent for females (Bank of Italy 2009, 95). When people know that no job is to be found, they give up looking for one. Thus, during a serious and prolonged crisis unemployment statistics generally show a downward bias.

7 Cf. Smith 1759, 162; Kant 1784, 130.

(technological, cultural, political and institutional) vicissitudes which marked their history.[8]

To sum up, each country grew more or less rapidly according to a set of conditions, in which there was nothing which forbade a quicker growth (or on the contrary, a slower growth or a decline). Migration between the different countries made up for the scarcity of labour power in those countries where economic growth was higher. When the problems grew more serious during wars, changes also came about in customs: in the early 1940s, during the Second World War, the USA registered a mass inflow of women into the labour market. The ecological problem itself is more a matter of the characteristics of growth than of the very possibilities of growth. Indeed, faster growth may provide the resources needed to tackle the problem better than slower growth can, and the culture of a country may attribute greater importance to the environment when the problems of poverty and unemployment do not loom large (even in a crisis like the present one, cases are not lacking of interventions aiming to support the economy and defend the environment at the same time, for instance with public support for investments in research on and development of less polluting energy sources).

The idea that economic growth follows a long-period equilibrium path is therefore an illusion, typical of those who conceive the economic issue as a problem of scarcity, with economic theory aiming at determining the conditions of equilibrium between supply and demand. Only from this point of view can the immediate path of the economy be interpreted as a matter of deviations in either direction, downwards or upwards, from an optimal path. As a matter of fact, the short-run movements of the economy contribute to determining its long-run evolution: a good rate of investments creates productive capacity and favours technical progress. We may thus have stages of growth or stagnation, or even decline, whose cumulative effects may be enormous. Argentina and Italy had a more or less similar per capita income between 1913 and 1950, however it then diverged until in 1987 Italian per capita income was three times that of Argentina (while the infant mortality rate in Argentina tripled the Italian rate).[9]

The separation between analysis of growth and analysis of the trade cycle – and hence interpretation of the crisis as the inevitable negative stage of the cycle, devoid of effects on the long run economic

---

8 For a less schematic illustration of the history of economic thought and of the comparison between the two main approaches, the scarcity-utility approach and the one focusing on the development of the division of labour, cf. Roncaglia 2001.

9 Cf. Roncaglia 1989. Innumerable examples of this kind may be found in *Contours of the World Economy, 1–2030 AD* by Angus Maddison (2007).

growth – has its roots in traditional mainstream theory, in the idea of a macroeconomic equilibrium between supply and demand determined by real variables alone, while the monetary variables determine (or contribute to determining) the trade cycle. Money lay behind inflation, while technology, saving propensity and readiness to work hard were taken to account for growth. The idea of a dichotomy between real and monetary variables was in fact strengthened in the 1980s with a particularly extreme form of confidence in the re-equilibrating forces of the market, namely the rational expectations approach. The main defect with this approach does not lie in the assumption that economic agents behave rationally, but in assuming that such rationality implies adoption, on the part of each and every economic agent, of the theory of economic equilibrium in the specific (and fallacious) variety of the existence, uniqueness and stability of a full employment equilibrium. It is precisely by adopting this view that the movements of the economy around the long period trend can only be attributed to unexpected shocks: it is only in this way, with uncritical adhesion to a theory by now happily discarded, that we can understand the repeated declarations of some mainstream economists (i.e. Perotti 2009) to the effect that we should not blame the economists for not having foreseen what was impossible to foresee.[10]

A different view of the role of money and finance was developed by Keynes and the post-Keynesian economists. As Keynes used to say, we live in a 'monetary production economy'. This means that the world of finance and that of production are interconnected: what happens in the first further influences events in the latter and vice versa. According to Keynes, indeed, the main influence goes from financial to real variables.

Let us consider how this may come about: here the Keynesian theory of uncertainty, discussed earlier, comes into play. We live in a world in which the different elements are characterized by different degrees of uncertainty. Therefore, economic agents find it convenient to keep a cushion of liquidity, namely something – money or other kinds of financial assets, starting with current account deposits (which precisely for this reason are often classified as money) – easy to sell, if unexpected events render this necessary or advantageous. All real assets (houses, gold, jewellery) are relatively more difficult to sell. Financial assets are also more or less liquid according to how readily they can be sold if needed and to the stability of their prices. For instance, shares of quoted

---

10 Similarly, in all probability it is confidence in the ability of market forces to re-equilibrate the economy which favours the optimism (noticed by Petrini 2009, 13–6; 34–5) shown in forecasts by the institutions of the Washington consensus and mainstream economists.

companies – the prices of which change from one moment to another – are less liquid than long term treasury bonds, and the latter are less liquid than treasury bills or short period bonds since the current prices of long term bonds are more sensitive than those of bills or short term bonds to changes in interest rates.

Increasing uncertainty determines a run to liquidity. In normal times, the monetary authorities can influence and exert a decisive influence on the availability of liquidity in financial markets through operations such as buying or selling treasury bills and bonds on the market. The preference for liquidity on the part of economic agents (and in particular of the largest among them, namely the banks and the other financial institutions) together with the policy of the monetary authorities determine the interest rate, which Keynes and the post-Keynesians consider as the price of liquidity. This theory is different from the traditional one, according to which the rate of interest is determined by demand and supply of loans (loanable funds theory) and thus ultimately by savings (which constitute the supply of loanable funds) and investments (demand). In comparison with these flows, the stock of financial activities cumulated at a given point in time is by far greater and can at any moment be reallocated between more and less liquid assets. Thus, the evolution of the financial markets depends on choices on the allocation of stocks of wealth between more or less liquid assets rather than on the path followed by saving and investment flows. Therefore Keynesian theory focuses attention on the preference for liquidity, which may change from one day to another in response not only to economic but also to political events in the widest sense of the term. Unlike the doctrine set out in mainstream economics textbooks, commonly following the so-called IS-LM scheme proposed by John Hicks (1937)[11], Keynes proposes a logical chain going from monetary and financial variables (with the determination of monetary interest rates based on liquidity preference) to the evolution of the real economy. We thus have, in logical sequel, interest rates, determined in monetary and financial markets, investments with decisions about them

---

11 In Hicks's scheme, the influence of monetary on real variables (through the influence on the rate of interest of the money supply and of the speculative demand for money, and the influence of the interest rate on investments and hence on income) is counterposed, within a general equilibrium scheme, to the influence of real on monetary variables (through the influence of income on the transaction demand for money). In other textbooks, macroeconomics is reduced to a theory of long-run growth (and an erroneous one, based as it is on the assumption of an inverse relation between real wage rate and demand for labour, which strictly speaking does not necessarily hold in a world with more than one commodity utilized as means of production), accompanied by analysis of the effects of real or monetary shocks (unforeseen events).

taken by comparing expected returns and financial conditions, income through the so-called multiplier, consumption. Indeed, the expression 'monetary production economy', utilized by Keynes in the preparatory stage of the *General Theory* (1936), stresses the prior role of money in accounting for economic events.

As defined by Adam Smith, the wealth of nations more or less corresponds to per capita income. Thus, it depends on the quantity of goods and services produced in the year. Economists differ not on this point but, as noted before, on the role of finance. According to mainstream economics, as we have seen earlier, financial factors may affect the trade cycle but not long period growth. According to Keynes and post-Keynesian economists, however, financial events exert an immediate influence on the path followed by investments and production which then translates, through the actual history of each economy, into a lasting influence.

All this means that it is important to guarantee good liquidity conditions for the economy as a whole, thus favouring the development of the financial markets. But it also means that it is of the utmost importance to avoid an abnormal development of these markets, which sooner or later but inevitably engenders a general collapse of the economy. We simply cannot believe that the markets will always find a stable equilibrium by themselves – or that the equilibrium determined within the financial markets, possibly with financial asset prices down by 50 per cent from a few days earlier, can be irrelevant for the real economy. As a consequence, the financial markets must be subjected to regulations aiming at making them as resilient as possible and the crises as undramatic as possible.

Regulations may apply to various aspects such as capital requirements for banks, for which the Basel rules should be improved upon, and also by extending them to all financial institutions: firstly, accounting rules (fair value, mark to market and other such rules so much under discussion recently) which should make the situation of financial institutions as transparent as possible, but which should also take better account of the need to avoid pro-cyclical effects, especially during stages of expansion (while under discussion now are ad hoc changes in aid of the financial institutions affected by the crisis, dangerously presenting such ad hoc changes as structural corrections, due to their convenience for the budgetary accounts of the financial institutions).[12] Secondly, adequate

---

12 For instance, this is the case of the transition from the rule of the mark to market criterion, which imposes recourse to market prices in the evaluation of assets in the banks' balance sheets, to the fair value criterion. This leaves to the institutions themselves greater freedom of choice between different criteria of evaluation. When financial crisis breaks out and the prices of financial assets plunge, in particular the prices of less liquid assets, the mark to market criterion

regulation of the derivatives markets and thirdly, laws to prevent the off-shore financial centres (the so-called regulatory havens) from making them inapplicable world-wide by evading regulations in a world where finance operates on a global scale. What matters is clarity about the limits of the market, side by side with recognition of its basic role in favouring the development of the division of labour and hence technical progress, which is the main source of economic and social development, together with its important role as precondition of political democracy.[13] An idealized view of the market, based on erroneous theories, leads to an erroneous interpretation of the present crisis, attractive – perhaps – precisely because it is edulcorated, but certainly also dangerous in view of the policy mistakes which it implied and implies.

---

amplifies the accounting oscillations of the active side of patrimonial accounts and thus of capital requirements computed according to the Basel rules. The shift to a fair value criterion therefore constitutes important help to avoid liquidity problems in a difficult moment, but in a boom stage it leaves the door open to the possibility of taking advantage of asset inflation in computing the capital available to meet the Basel requirements. Hence, there would be a structural slackening of the regulations on the capital requirements of banks and only to a limited degree, as far as the negative stages of the trade cycle are concerned, a reduction in the pro-cyclical effects of the regulations.

13 To maintain that the market is an imperfect institution does not mean denigrating it, and certainly not supporting a centrally planned economy. It is precisely in order to defend the market and draw from it the economic and political advantages it can offer, that it is important to recognize the thesis of the 'invisible hand of the market' as a myth, in the twofold meaning that it is wrong to attribute it to Adam Smith and that, at the theoretical level, the thesis of a system-wide intrinsic stability of the market mechanisms is wrong. *Il mito della mano invisibile* (The myth of the invisible hand) is the theme (and the title) of a recent work of mine (cf. Roncaglia 2005).

8

A New Bretton Woods?

At the moment, policy appears to be doing better than it did at the time of the Great Crash nearly a century ago, as far as the issue of unemployment is concerned. This is certainly no small result. However, we should also take into account the difficulties which might arise over the sustainability of public and external debts. The real issue, though, concerns the need to deal adequately with regulation of the economy and particularly of finance. The changes we have seen over the past four decades in the functioning of the market economy have been enormous, and we cannot believe that a simple return to the rules prevailing at the time of the 'economic miracle' of the 1950s and 1960s is a feasible strategy. More importantly, given the global nature of the economy as well as of finance, if we are to prevent the new regulations from being undermined by the persistence of regulatory havens, there are formidable tasks to be tackled to build a new world economic order. In this respect, many commentators have referred to the need for 'a new Bretton Woods' (from the name of the US town where agreement was reached on the post-war international monetary system in 1944). As a matter of fact, the issues are at least partly different from those then at centre stage, and apply in particular to a wider spectrum of issues. These should therefore be tackled in a coordinated way but along different paths: the search for a global solution, which could solve all problems at once, may prove too difficult – practically impossible – and thus turn out to be counterproductive.

Let us attempt an overview of the main issues for the policy agenda to tackle the crisis, starting with the most immediate ones.

As we have seen, governments have learned from the experience of past crises and are now ready to support global demand with fiscal and monetary interventions, fully aware of the importance of responding to the crisis of confidence.[1] The central banks have

---

1 In Italy, blessed with a media oriented government, the policy of supporting confidence acquired such extreme connotations as to fall into ridicule and be counterproductive, with critiques, reminiscent of Mussolini's times, of the defeatism of the media and veiled threats to the top managers of public institutions responsible for providing official statistics or producing forecasts,

channelled enormous quantities of liquidity into the economy, thus driving down the interest rates with extreme determination, as indeed was certainly necessary. This has been the case in Europe, to the extent that many countries went much further than the limits set for budget deficits by the Maastricht rules. The new US President Obama also announced a package of public interventions in support of the economy. China did likewise, with an extensive programme of investments in infrastructures. If China and India go on growing fast enough, even if somewhat slowed down from the recent past, the crisis could be milder and shorter in the Western countries as well, but at the same time there will be a significant redistribution of power equilibriums in the world economy.

However, these measures imply increasing public deficits and consequent expansion of public debts. Thus, when the worst of the crisis is behind us (in terms of production and employment, not of share prices in the stock exchange!), we may expect renewed importance for the target of limiting public deficits and the public debt, though at the cost of slowing down growth. In Italy, this problem will be more severe than elsewhere since this country has a public debt well above the European average. Some experts foresee in this respect an inflationary upsurge[2] since this is a traditional tool for reducing the weight of the public debt. Such an outcome is considered more likely because of the weight acquired by the public debt in the recent past, to the extent that it may be difficult to reduce it gradually by re-establishing a positive sign for the difference between income and expenditure in the public accounts (which is also made more difficult because of the increase in the expenditure for interest on debt). Firms, too, could find an inflationary

---

especially whenever these did not fall into line with the official optimism of the government: as if the present crisis were not real, but only depended on a pessimistic view of reality.

2 In various cases forecasts of this kind are vitiated by the underlying monetarist view which links the path of prices to the money supply. As a matter of fact, the very rapid increase in the monetary base on the part of the central banks has been absorbed by the explosive growth of the demand for liquidity on the part of the financial institutions and the public in general, while prices have been pushed downward by the situation of excess supply in many markets, in particular for raw materials. Indeed, the rhetoric on inflation from money supply expansion has been utilized, in non-competitive markets, as a justification for unwarranted price increases. We may add, however, that the presence of an enormous mass of liquidity in search of profitable employment may translate into an upward pressure on prices in futures markets for raw commodities. This, in the presence of oligopolistic markets, may have a contagion effect on spot prices, independently of the path followed by demand and supply, as already seems to be happening.

upsurge advantageous because of the reduction it would bring about in the value of private debts. On the whole, if the crisis should turn out to be shorter and milder thanks to public interventions, the successive upturn may prove to be slower and less vigorous, and accompanied by a host of problems.[3]

Within a general expansionary policy drive, there are various choices to be made, each having some advantages and some disadvantages. Measures in support of private consumption may be obtained through subsidies to families through reduction of the fiscal burden on families or through reduction of indirect taxes on commodity goods and services. In order to have noticeable effects in a situation of heavy crisis, these measures should be very extensive. Moreover, they should be framed in such a way as to favour the poorer strata of the population, not only for reasons of equity, which should be sufficient in themselves, but also for reasons of efficacy. Economic theory indicates that a shift of resources from the more to the less wealthy favours the growth of consumption since the poor spend a higher proportion of their income than the rich. General tax abatement is thus likely to be less effective than other measures.

An increase in consumption would help as a stimulus to investments, but risks favouring, at least in part, imports and not only internal production. Of course, one country's imports are other countries' exports, and coordinated measures in support of consumption taken by a good number of countries have an expansionary effect on all. However, the distribution of advantages stemming from such measures depends significantly on the competitiveness of the different countries. In this respect, Italy shows serious signs of deterioration, thus requiring ad hoc measures such as those discussed in the following concerning investments in research and in education.

It seems less reasonable to have extensive recourse to abatement of taxes. This is a measure that can be framed in such a way as to be advantageous in particular for firms or for families. In the former case, the main target would be a stimulus to investments, in the latter a

---

3 For now, the main risk of an uncontrolled expansion of the public debt – which is often accompanied by an expansion of the external debt – is a debt crisis in some of the more exposed countries. Even if the crisis should be limited to two or three smaller countries (the more likely candidates appear to be some ex-communist countries), thus avoiding the risks of a widespread contagion, it would lead to a marked increase in interest spreads on public debt of different countries. This would have an impact on the public accounts of the countries involved which would be all the stronger the greater the ratio of debt to national income, with the risk of bringing about an explosively spiralling increase in the public deficit and increase in public and external debt in various other countries.

stimulus to consumption. However, in the former case the effects would be limited by doubts on the part of the entrepreneurs as to there being sufficient demand for their products. In the current situation what firms would save on taxes they would redirect to financial use, if not directly to an increase in liquidity reserves. In the latter case, if the tax rebate were distributed over all levels of income, the effects on consumption would be rather modest and in any case less than obtainable with measures of support targeting the less wealthy families.

What is hard to understand is why coordinated large scale investment projects such as those required for an abatement of pollution should be sacrificed in order to leave room for tax rebates. This idea was initially defended by many commentators and for a certain period by the Italian government as well, to be rapidly abandoned when confronted with Obama's decision to go ahead with strong anti-pollution measures at the G8 meeting at L'Aquila on 9 July 2009.[4] As a matter of fact, public investments aiming at this target are precisely the kind of measures that should be implemented in times of crisis, as President Obama maintained. These are measures which stimulate employment, although strictly defined not necessarily within the government sector. Indeed these measures apply to the implementation of infrastructures of different kinds, generally entrusted to companies on the borderline between the private and the public sector, from railways to city transport, from sewer systems to garbage treatments and disposal plants. The effects on the economy of public expenditure to hire workers for such projects are greater than the effects of personal income support measures. This is due to the fact that higher family incomes are only in part utilized for consumption expenditure. Keynes remarked, that in times of crisis a positive stimulus to the economy can even come from digging holes in the ground only to fill them in subsequently (as the Americans did in fact with highly sophisticated equipment in the Korean war, then in Vietnam and in Iraq). However, it is certainly better to use public expenditure to do something useful. To this end, he proposed that the government should have investment projects in infrastructure ready to be implemented in periods of crisis.[5]

Expansion of public investments in research and development of new technologies would be still more useful. However, together with public expenditure on education, these seem to be the first victims of

---

4 'Let us make it clear: if exit from the crisis in 2010 should mean to pollute yet another year at current rates, let us do so' (Alesina 2009; online, author's translation).

5 Cf. Guger and Walterskirchen 1988. Obviously this does not mean foregoing evaluation of comparative utility among the various projects.

policies to curb public spending. In particular the Italian economy, although it felt the impact of the financial crisis less than the Anglo-Saxon countries or other countries with a similar financial structure, has been hit hard by the economic crisis. This should be seen in the light of the fact that Italy has shown productivity dynamics systematically inferior to those of the other EU countries in the recent past, foreboding a relatively long period of decline for the Italian economy.

In any case, the main interventions should be of an institutional kind, aiming at providing the foundations for a less fragile market economy. The issues to tackle concern, among other things, the system of financial regulations, reform of the international monetary system, competition policies and defence of the environment.

The need for a robust regulatory system for financial activities is, by now, very clear, and many working groups, at both the national and the international level, are already at work. In this respect, the activities of the Financial Stability Board (the former Financial Stability Forum) chaired by the Governor of the Bank of Italy, Mario Draghi, are very important. Not only banks, but the whole of the financial sector needs regulating: regulatory segmentation between the different typologies of financial institutions should be considerably reduced.[6] International agreements are decisive to avoid repetition of what we have seen in the past: competition from the havens of unregulated finance (which by and large correspond to tax havens) rendering any national attempt at regulation vain.[7] Indeed, in the Bush era competition from regulatory havens was utilized as a justification in support of deregulatory policies in the financial sector: those policies which, as is now recognized by nearly all, have had so much responsibility for the crisis. If there were a common will, it would be very simple to set rules to isolate those countries, for instance with fiscal disincentives for institutions choosing them as their base. The obligation could be introduced (with attention to its implementation where it already holds in principle) to notify the national monetary and tax authorities of all transactions with persons or entities having domicile in those countries as counterparts, while excluding deducibility for tax purposes of any payment effected through transfer of funds towards such countries and considering as taxable income all funds received from them. Any agreement, having

---

6 'If it quacks like a bank, regulate it like a bank' (Kuttner 2008, online). For some proposals drawing on Minsky's theories cf. Montanaro and Tonveronachi 2009c.

7 At the end of 2007, the Cayman Islands hosted more than 80 per cent of the then active hedge funds.

as counterpart a subject based in those countries, should be declared automatically void. It is not the tools for intervention that are lacking; what has been lacking, at least up to now, is the will to intervene.

In a US Congressional hearing in October 2008, Joseph Stiglitz criticized the stock options for finance managers which constitute an incentive to misleading accounting and proposed, among other things, the elimination of off-balance-sheet transactions, more severe rules on conflicts of interest and against the risks of regulatory capture (in particular on the 'revolving door' practice by which controllers and controlled continually change place and role), substitution of private rating agencies with a government agency, prohibition of variable rate mortgages in which amortization instalments are excessively volatile and changes in the preferential fiscal treatment for capital gains.

The international monetary system also generated disequilibriums which had an important role in determining conditions for the crisis. When a new Bretton Woods is mooted, reference is to the rules of the international monetary system agreed on in 1944 which favoured development of international economic relations and thus development of the world economy up to the 1971 crisis. Based on a system of official exchange rates, with an active controlling role attributed to the International Monetary Fund, the system differed from the one proposed by Keynes in that it was based on the dollar (convertible in gold on request from other countries' central banks at a pre-set exchange rate), rather than a new international currency to be issued by the IMF, the bancor. When, with the Vietnam War, the USA accumulated balance of payments deficits of proportions notably greater than their gold reserves, the Bretton Woods system plunged into crisis. The then President of the USA, Nixon, unilaterally proclaimed the full unpegging of the dollar from gold on 15 August 1971. After some attempts at putting back on its feet an international monetary system based on fixed exchange rates, a system of free-floating exchange rates was adopted to the great joy of the supporters of extreme *laissez-faire*. Instability was thereby increased. Moreover, given that the dollar in any case remained the core currency of the system, the deficits in the US balance of payments could be accommodated, thus escaping the need for immediate adjustment measures. Actually, the disequilibrium situation has worsened over the past decade: countries with a strongly active balance of payments, such as China, have accumulated gigantic dollar reserves. As we have seen, management of these reserves was partly attributed to sovereign investment funds. Given their dimensions, the mixture of political and economic elements in their investment choices and their very poor transparency, such funds may heavily condition international economic relations and bring about distortions in important markets, putting an unhealthy distance between them and normal competitive conditions.

The pure and simple return to the structure of the international monetary system proposed by Keynes is impossible precisely because in international transactions the short and very short-run financial movements by far dominate over those concerning commercial transactions and direct investments.[8] If we wish to reduce the fragility of the international financial system, reform of the international monetary system cannot be divorced from the regulation of financial activities.[9] However, in order to take some steps forward in these directions, it may be better to tackle the two issues separately, coming to reform of the international monetary system subsequent to addressing new rules for international and national financial activities. What is rather worrying is the dilatory approach to the latter issue and the resistance to change represented both by the interests which would be hit by a new and stronger set of regulations and by the very strong ideological and cultural residues of the Washington consensus.[10]

Other issues interact with those concerning the international monetary and financial system. Let us recall two of them: environmental policies, again to the fore thanks to the change of perspective brought in by President Obama, may – as we have already seen – constitute a priority target, together with expenditure on research and development of new technologies, in choosing how to allocate public expenditure in support of the economy.

The second issue concerns competition policies. These should constitute an important part of reform of the rules of the economic game, and all the more so if they should be the object of international cooperation. This applies in particular to energy sources such as oil and natural gas, where financial speculation may have operated side by side with policies of implicit collusion on the part of the sector's major companies. As a consequence, this has generated considerable price instability with negative

---

8　Cf. Kregel 2009b. Some of Keynes's specific proposals rather appear to retain relevance today, which is the case of the creation of a supranational bank and currency (cf. Alessandrini and Fratianni 2009).

9　Without entering into the vast and complex discussion that arose, we may recall here the 'Keynesian' proposal advanced by James Tobin, Nobel prize winner in 1981, to tax (at a very low rate) currency transactions so as to hinder speculative operations (cf. Tobin 1974; Eichengreen, Tobin and Wyplosz 1995). Obviously, if all currency dealings were to take place between agents all registered at the Cayman Islands, the Tobin tax would become a further incentive favouring tax havens.

10　For more cf., however, United Nations 2009.

effects for the planning of investments, both in these sectors and in those of alternative energy sources, and indeed in terms of destabilizing effects on the world economy.[11] A coordinated policy on the part of the major consumer and producer countries might also have an important positive effect on international economic relations, reducing the risk of economic tensions going on to fuel political and military tensions as well.

---

11 The development of Brent and West Texas Intermediate markets – two varieties of crude oil of which one counts for less than one per cent of international trade and the other is not traded internationally at all since it remains within the US market – has been dominated by the financial/speculative component: future contracts dominate over spot dealings to the measure of 100 to one, with completely opaque markets (declaring the terms of contracts is optional, and there is no sanction for false declarations). The use of this market for price indexation in the agreements for crude oil long period sales is a total absurdity which can be explained only by the opportunity it provides for implicit collusion among sellers. The influx of financial resources into these markets, moreover, entailed a strong upward boost to prices, utterly devoid of meaning from the point of view of the 'fundamentals' of oil production and consumption (cf. Roncaglia 2003). For the proposal of a buffer stock for the stabilization of oil prices cf. Roncaglia 1991.

9

The Future of Capitalism

The issue of regulations which concerns both the financial markets and the international monetary system on the one hand, and environment and competition policies on the other, brings us to the broader issue raised by the financial and economic crisis: what are the prospects for the market economy? Should we fear, as some maintain, or hope, as others suggest, that the market economy will be superseded?

As Giorgio Ruffolo (*Il capitalismo ha i secoli contati*, 2008) pithily put it, 'capitalism has but a few centuries of residual life': its disappearance is not around the corner, especially after the discouraging experience of planned economies, unless we foresee growing instability for the world economy with economic tensions which could in turn generate unsustainable social, political and military tensions. However, it is clear that tomorrow's capitalism will be different from today's, but in what respects?

Let us distinguish two tendencies which have characterized recent decades: globalization and financialization. The latter bears a large part of the responsibility for economic instability and the crisis. In this respect, let us point out once again, the need is for a radical change of route: not in the direction of administrative interventions or acquisition of the major banks on the part of the state, but in the direction of clear and transparent rules, applicable to all market operators. Rather, globalization needs to be subdivided into its two components. Firstly, we have the growth of world economic interdependence, which applies to the international division of labour and implies a drive to technological progress.[1] Secondly, we have international expansion of the financial markets which has positive aspects (mainly concerning long-term capital movements) and negative ones (mainly concerning short and very short-term capital movements – those which Keynes wanted to constrain with his programme for a new international monetary system, only partially implemented with the Bretton Woods agreements). Protectionist reactions to the crisis,

---

1 Amartya Sen (2002) put great stress on this aspect, pointing out among other things that it is not necessarily opposed to policies aiming at favouring an economic growth compatible with the growth of solidarity relations within the local communities.

fortunately avoided so far by the overwhelming majority of countries, would directly hit the international division of labour. Moreover, they would signal the choice of national responses to the crisis, which would frustrate attempts to reach a reasoned out international consensus over setting common rules for international economic relations. Rules agreed on by a sufficiently large group of countries are needed to avoid downward competition between national regulatory schemes: downward competition systematically utilized by the supporters of deregulation, in absence of the will to apply discriminatory measures against tax and regulatory havens.

Growing income inequality within the major countries over the two decades characterized by the growth of unregulated finance marks the main difficulty on the road to the adoption of new rules designed to endow the growth of a free market economy with stability. As for the adoption of stringent competition and environmental policies, regulation of financial activity, too, hits interest groups which, though weakened on account of the crisis, are still powerful and thus able to influence the cultural debate and policy choices. It is precisely for this reason that it is important to be clear about the erroneousness of some commonplace tenets like the myth of the invisible hand of the market or the Washington consensus view of the working of the economy, utilized in defence of policies which, while creating the conditions for crisis to break out, also served to increase the inequality of income distribution.

Classical authors like Adam Smith and John Stuart Mill had stressed the distinction between selfishness and self-interest and hence the need for an adequate system of rules – not only laws, but also customs dictated by common morality – which, within the complex system of passions and interests directing human actions, could direct individuals to take into account the needs and hopes of other members of society.[2] The market economy does not operate in a void: it operates within a political and social set-up which interacts with it in different ways. Thus, the economic crisis will have heavy repercussions with increasing social tensions that can only be avoided with close attention to the costs of the crisis itself for the lower strata of society. This means countering the crisis in a long period perspective, taking steps to reinforce social cohesion with measures to enhance efficiency in the administration of justice and the formative activities of public education, both vital to reverse the decline in moral behaviour which characterizes so many countries today.

---

2 Cf. Roncaglia 2001, chapters 5 and 8.

Bibliography

Author's Note: The year after the author's name indicates the original publication date. Page references in the text refer to the last published editions quoted in the following. When it is not an English edition, the translation of the passages quoted in the text is mine.

Alesina A. 2009. "Il Falso e Vero Verde del Nuovo Sviluppo." *Il Sole 24 Ore* (28 April 2009).

Alesina A. and F. Giavazzi. 2008. *La crisi*. Milano: Il Saggiatore.

Alessandrini P. and M. Fratianni. 2009. "Resurrecting Keynes to Stabilize the International Monetary System", *Open Economies Review* 20, no. 3: 339–58.

Amari G. 2009. "Postfazione". In G. Amari and N. Rocchi (eds). *Federico Caffè. Un Economista per il Nostro Tempo*. Roma: Ediesse, 1043–1131.

Babbage C. 1832. *On the Economy of Machinery and Manufactures*. London: Charles Knight. Reprint of the fourth edition (1835). New York: M. Kelley.

Bank for International Settlements. 2009. *79a Relazione Annuale*. Basilea.

Bank of Italy. 2009. *Relazione Annuale*. Roma.

Bank of England. 2007. *Financial Stability Report*. London.

Bernoulli J. 1713. *Ars Conjectandi*. Thurmisiorum: Basilea.

Biasco S. 1987. "Currency Cycles and the International Economy". *BNL Quarterly Review* 40, no. 160: 31–60.

———— 1988. "Dynamic and Incapsulating Processes in the Generation of the World Demand". *BNL Quarterly Review* 41, no. 165, 179–215.

Boyer R. 2009. "Feu le Régime d'Accumulation Tiré par la Finance". *Revue de la Régulation*, no. 5. Online: http://regulation.revues.org/index7367.html

Caffè F. 1976. "Economia di Mercato e Socializzazione delle Sovrastrutture Finanziarie" in Caffè F. *Un'Economia in Ritardo*. Torino: Boringhieri, 17–47. Reprinted in G. Amari and N. Rocchi (eds). *Federico Caffè. Un Economista per gli Uomini Comuni*. Roma: Ediesse 2007, 237–53.

Cobianchi M. 2009. *Bluff*. Milano: orme editori.

Consumer Federation Foundation. 2009. *Sold-out: How Wall Street and Washington Betrayed America*. Online: www.wallstreetwatch.org

Cooper G. 2008. *The Origin of Financial Crises*. New York: Vintage Books.

De Finetti B. 1930. "Fondamenti Logici del Ragionamento Probabilistico." *Bollettino dell'Unione Matematica Italiana* 9, 258–61.

———— 1931. *Probabilismo. Saggio Critico sulla Teoria della Probabilità e sul Valore della Scienza*. Napoli: Perrella.

De Finetti B. and F. Emanuelli. 1967. *Economia delle Assicurazioni*. Torino: Utet.

Eichengreen B., Tobin J. et al. 1995. "The Case for Sand in the Wheels of International Finance". *Economic Journal* 105, no. 428,162–72.

Giavazzi F. 2009. "Allarmare non Paga". *Corriere della Sera*. (3 March 2009).

Godley W. and A. Izurieta. 2004. "The US Economy: Weaknesses if the 'Strong' Recovery." *BNL Quarterly Review* 57, no. 229, 131–9.

Godley W., Papadimitriou D. et al. 2007. *The U.S. Economy: Is There a Way out of the Woods?*. Strategic Analysis. Annandale-on-Hudson: The Levy Economics Institute.

Godley W., Papadimitriou D. et al. 2008. *Prospects of the United States and the World: a Crisis that Conventional Remedies Cannot Resolve*. Strategic Analysis. Annandale-on-Hudson: The Levy Economics Institute.

Greenspan A. 2009. "We need a Better Cushion Against Risk." *Financial Times*. Supplement on *The future of Capitalism. The Big Debate* (12 May 2009).

Guger A. and E. Walterskirchen. 1988. "Fiscal and Monetary Policy in the Keynes-Kalecki Tradition". In J. A. Kregel, E. Matzner et al. (eds). *Barriers to Full Employment*. Basingstoke: Macmillan, 103–32.

Hall P. A. and D. Soskice. 2001. *Varieties of Capitalism. The Institutional Foundations of Comparative Advantage*. Oxford: Oxford University Press.

Harcourt G. C. 1972. *Some Cambridge Controversies in the Theory of Capital*. Cambridge: Cambridge University Press.

Hicks J. 1937. "Mr. Keynes and the Classics: a Suggested Interpretation". *Econometrica* 5, no. 2, 147–59.

Kaldor N. and J. Mirrlees. 1962. "A New Model of Economic Growth". *Review of Economic Studies* 29, 174–92.

Kant I. 1784. "Idee zu einer allgemeinen Geschichte in Weltbürgerlicher Absicht". *Berlinische Monatsschrift* 4, 385–411. Italian translation "Idea di una Storia Universale dal Punto di Vista Cosmopolitico". In I. Kant. *Scritti Politici*. Torino: Utet 1956. third ed. 1995, 123–39.

Keynes J. M. 1921. *A Treatise on Probability*. London: Macmillan. Reprinted in J. M. Keynes. *Collected Writings*, vol. 8. London: Macmillan 1973.

———— 1931. "Ramsey as a philosopher". *The New Statesman and Nation*. (3 October 1931). Reprinted in *Essays in Biography*. In J. M. Keynes. *Collected Writings*, vol. 10. London: Macmillan 1972, 335–46.

———— 1936. *The General Theory of Employment, Interest and Money*. London: Macmillan. Reprinted in J. M. Keynes. *Collected Writings*, vol. 7. London: Macmillan 1973.

Kindleberger C. P. 1973. *The World in Depression, 1929–1939*. Berkeley and Los Angeles: University of California Press.

———— 1978. *Manias, Panics and Crashes. A History of Financial Crisis*. New York: Basic Books.

———— 1995. "Asset Inflation and Monetary Policy", *BNL Quarterly Review* 48, no. 192: 17–37.

———— 2002. "The Price Level of Monetary Policy." *BNL Quarterly Review* 55, no. 220: 3–12.

Knight F. M. 1921. *Risk, Uncertainty and Profit*. Boston: Houghton Mifflin.

Kregel J. 2007. "The Natural Instability of Financial Markets". *Working Paper* 523. Annandale-on-Hudson: The Levy Economics Institute.

Bibliography

Kregel J. 2008. "Minsky's Cushions of Safety". *Public Policy Brief* 93, Annandale-on-Hudson: The Levy Economics Institute.

Kregel J. 2009a. "Managing the Impact of Volatility in International Capital Markets in an Uncertain World". *Working Paper* 558. Annandale-on-Hudson: The Levy Economics Institute.

―――― "Some Simple Observations on the Reform of the International Monetary System" – *Policy Note* 8. Annandale-on-Hudson: The Levy Economics Institute.

Kuczynski P. and J. Williamson (eds). 2003. *After the Washington Consensus*. Washington: Institute for International Economics.

Kuttner R. 2008. "Seven Deadly Sins of Deregulation and Three Necessary Reforms." *The American Prospect* (17 September 2008).

Maddison A. 2007. *Contours of the World Economy, 1–2030 AD*. Oxford: Oxford University Press.

Malkiel B. G. and A. Saha. 2005. "Hedge Funds: Risk and Return." *Financial Analysts Journal* 61, no. 6: 80–8.

Minsky H. P. 1975. *John Maynard Keynes*. New York: Columbia University Press.

―――― 1982. *Can 'It' Happen Again? Essays on Instability and Finance*. Armonk (N.Y.): Sharpe.

―――― 1993. "Schumpeter and Finance". In S. Biasco, A. Roncaglia et al. (eds). *Market and Institutions in Economic Development. Essays in Honour of Paolo Sylos Labini*. London: Macmillan, 103–15.

Montanaro E. and M. Tonveronachi. 2009a. "Il Secondo Pilastro di Basilea 2. Prove di Stress per le Banche o per la Vigilanza?" *Banca Impresa Società* 28, no. 1: 71–91.

―――― 2009b. "Rischio di Liquidità, Crisi Bancarie e Regolamentazione: Nuove Prospettive". In *Banche e Sistema Finanziario: Vecchie Questioni e Problematiche Attuali. Saggi in Onore di Francesco Cesarini*, Bologna: Il Mulino, 83–101.

―――― 2009c. "Some Preliminary Proposals for Re-regulating Financial Systems". *Quaderni del Dipartimento di Economia Politica* 553. Siena: Università degli Studi.

Morris C. 2008. *The Trillion Dollar Meltdown*. New York: Public Affairs.

Neumann J. Von and O. Morgenstern. 1944. *Theory of Games and Economic Behaviour*. Princeton: Princeton University Press. Second edition 1947; third edition 1953.

Perotti R. 2009. "Economisti alla Sbarra, Ecco L'atto di Accusa." *Il Sole 24 Ore* (27 May 2009).

Petrini R. 2009. *Processo agli Economisti*. Milano: Chiarelettere.

Quadrio Curzio A. and V. Miceli. 2009. *I Fondi Sovrani*. Bologna: il Mulino.

Rajan R. G. and L. Zingales. 2003. *Saving Capitalism from the Capitalists*. New York: Random House.

Rampini F. 2009. *Le Dieci Cose che Non Saranno Più le Stesse*. Milano: Arnoldo Mondadori Editore.

Ramsey F. 1931. *The Foundations of Mathematics*. London: Routledge & Kegan Paul.

Roncaglia A. 1989. "Italian Economic Growth: A Smithian View". *Quaderni di Storia dell'Economia Politica* 7, no. 2–3: 227–34.

_____ 1991. "La Stabilizzazione Del Prezzo del Petrolio: Alcuni Commenti". *Economia delle Fonti di Energia* 34, no. 44: 71–8.

_____ 2001. *La Ricchezza delle Idee*. Roma-Bari: Laterza. English edition *The Wealth of Economic Ideas*. Cambridge: Cambridge University Press 2005.

_____ 2003. "Energy and Market Power: an Alternative Approach to the Economics of Oil." *Journal of Post Keynesian Economics* 25, 641–59.

_____ 2005. *Il Mito della Mano Invisibile*. Roma-Bari: Laterza.

_____. 2006. "Tasa de Desempleo y Tasas de Empleo: Categorias Estadisticas o Construcciones Teoricas?" *Investigacion Economica* 65, no. 257: 45–61.

_____ 2009a. *Piero Sraffa*. Basingstoke: Palgrave Macmillan.

_____. 2009b. "Keynes and Probability: an Assessment". *European Journal of the History of Economic Thought* 16, no. 3: 489–510.

Roncaglia A. and P. Sylos Labini. 1995. *Il Pensiero Economico. Temi e Protagonisti*. Roma-Bari: Laterza.

Rothschild E. 2001. *Economic Sentiments. Adam Smith, Condorcet and the Enlightenment*. Cambridge (Mass.): Harvard University Press.

Roubini N. 2009. "Le Meravigliose Bolle di Sapone 'Carry Trade'". *Il Sole 24 Ore* (3 November 2009).

Ruffolo G. 2008. *Il Capitalismo ha i Secoli Contati*. Torino: Einaudi.

Sarcinelli M. 2003. "Crisi Economiche e Mercati Finanziari: è di Aiuto un Nuovo Ordine Finanziario?" *Moneta e Credito* 56, no. 224: 387–422.

Savage L. J. 1954. *The Foundation of Statistics*. New York: Wiley.

Schumpeter J. 1912. *Theorie der Wirtschaftlichen Entwicklung*. München-Leipzig: Duncker & Humblot. English edition *The Theory of Economic Development*. Cambridge (Mass.): Harvard University Press 1934.

Sciandra L. 2008. "I Derivati degli Enti Locali: Origine, Dimensione e Criticità". In *Finanza Pubblica e Istituzioni*. Rapporto ISAE, Maggio, Roma: Istituto di Studi e Analisi Economica.

Sen A. 2002. *Globalizzazione e Libertà*. Milano: Mondadori.

Shiller R. J. 2008. *The Subprime Solution*. Princeton: Princeton University Press.

Smith A. 1759. *The Theory of Moral Sentiments*. London: A. Millar. Critical edition, D.D. Raphael and A.L. Macfie (eds). Oxford: Oxford University Press 1976.

Smith A. 1776. *An Inquiry Into the Nature and Causes of the Wealth of Nations*. London: W. Strahan and T. Cadell. Critical edition, R. H. Campbell and A. S. Skinner (eds). Oxford: Oxford University Press 1976.

Soros G. 1999. *The Crisis of Global Capitalism. Open Society Endangered*. New York: Public Affairs.

Soros G. 2002. *Globalization*. New York: Public Affairs.

_____ 2008a. *The New Paradigm for Financial Markets*. New York: Public Affairs.

_____ 2008b. "The Crisis and What to Do About It". *The New York Review of Books* 55, no. 19 (4 December 2008).

Sraffa P. 1960. *Production of Commodities by Means of Commodities*. Cambridge: Cambridge University Press.

Stiglitz J. 2008. "Testimony" to the Committee on Financial Services, U. S. House of Representatives, Online: http://www.house-gov/financialservices/hearing110/hr102108.shtml.

Bibliography

Sylos Labini P. 1984. *The Forces of Economic Growth and Decline.* Cambridge (Mass.): MIT Press.

Sylos Labini P. 2003. "Prospects for the World Economy". *BNL Quarterly Review* 56, no. 226: 179–206.

Tabellini G. 2009. "Il Mondo Dopo la Prima Crisi Globale." *Il Sole 24 Ore* (7 May 2009).

Taleb N. N. 2008. *The Black Swan. The Impact of the Highly Improbable.* New York: Random House.

Tobin J. 1974. *The New Economy One Decade Older.* The Janeway Lectures on Historical Economics. Princeton: Princeton University Press.

Tonveronachi M. 1983. *J. M. Keynes. Dall'Instabilità Ciclica all'Equilibrio di Sottoccupazione.* Roma: La Nuova Italia Scientifica.

Tonveronachi M. 2007. "Implications of Basel II for Financial Stability. Clouds are Darker for Developing Countries". *BNL Quarterly Review* 60, no. 241: 111–35.

Tremonti G. 2008. *La Paura e la Speranza.* Milano: Mondadori.

United Nations. 2009. Report of the Commission of Experts of the President of the United Nations General Assembly on Reforms of the International Monetary and Financial System. Preliminary version. Online: www.un.org/ga/president/63/interactive/financialcrisis/PreliminaryReport210509.pdf

Williamson J. 1990. "What Washington Means by Policy Reform". In J. Williamson (ed.). *Latin American Adjustment. How Much Has Happened?* Washington, DC: Institute for International Economics.

Breinigsville, PA USA
29 October 2010
248209BV00001BA/4/P